good cooking

Cooking for All Seasons

Published by:

R&R Publications Marketing Pty. Ltd

ACN 083 612 579

PO Box 254, Carlton North, Victoria 3054 Australia

Phone (61 3) 9381 2199 Fax (61 3) 9381 2689

E-mail: info@randrpublications.com.au

Web: www.randrpublications.com.au

©Richard Carroll

Good Cooking Cooking for All Seasons

Publisher: Richard Carroll

Creative Director: Lucy Adams

Production Manager: Anthony Carroll

Computer Graphics: Lucy Adams

Food Photography: Steve Baxter, Phillip Wilkins, David Munns, Thomas Odulate, Christine Hanscomb, Gary Smith, Warren Webb, and Frank Wieder

Home Economist: Sara Buenfeld, Emma Patmore, Nancy McDougall, Louise Pickford, Jane Stevenson, Oded Schwartz, Alison Austin, and Jane Lawrie

Food Stylists: Helen Payne, Sue Russell, Sam Scott, Antonia Gaunt Ellen Argyriou, and Oded Schwartz

Recipe Development: Terry Farris, Jacqueline Bellefontaine, Ellen Argyriou Becky Johnson, Valerie Barrett, Emma Patmore, Geri Richards, Pam Mallender, Jan Fullwood and Tanara Milstein (www.tamaraskitchen.com.) pages 58, 64 and 262.

Nutritional Consultant: Moya de Wet BSc SRD

Proof Reader: Fiona Brodribb

Includes Index

ISBN 1 74022 223 7

EAN 9 781740 22223 5

First Edition Printed September 2003

Computer Typeset in Times New Roman, Verdana, Helvetica, Shelley Allegro & Humanist

Printed in Singapore by Saik Wah Press Pte Ltd

good cooking

Contents

Cooking for All Seasons

Introduction

Spring

Spring arrives – always – just in time. Despite a lingering chill in the air, we don sweaters and running shoes and head outdoors. Windows get washed, driveways are swept, and lawns are raked as everyone says goodbye to the remains of winter. Welcome this warm weather with some of the light, simple recipes we've put together for the spring season.

Summer

Summer is hot, and the pace changes. It's a time of year to keep things simple and cool, so many of us plan our meals around the barbecue. Appetites grow smaller and main course salads become popular alterntaives to heavier meals. If you'd like a little adventure in outdoor cooking, then look through our selection of recipes created for the open campfire. Take a moment to read our recipe ideas in the Summer section, and you may find just the right combination of dishes that you are looking for.

Fall

The draining heat seems to disappear overnight with the chilly winds of Fall. Appetites return and everyone's first instinct is to head indoors and eat. This is when we can fill the house with scents of fresh bread, chowders, and baked pies. Inside our Autumn section are some recipes that might inspire you to turn the last vegetables and fruits into some thing great.

Winter

When winter blows in, it truly gets cold, and we all try to forget about the bitter winds and frozen ears! We turn to things that bring us warmth and comfort. It's the time of year to take comfort in tempting casseroles, and soul-warming soups. Enjoy this selection of winter recipes, along with some festive menu ideas for the season.

The blossoms are out, the landscape is turning green, and it's time to shed those winter layers and come out of hibernation. Make the most of the fresh seasonal ingredients which include apricots, artichokes, asparagus, broccoli, brussels sprouts, ginger, grapes, mangoes, new potatoes, pineapple, rhubarb, spinach, strawberries, and sugar snap peas. In this section you'll find some light spring appetizers, including Artichokes Braised in White Wine; some great fish dishes, such as Griddled Scallops with Orange Salsa; and a variety of sweet baked goods, including Hot Brownies with White Chocolate Sauce.

Spring

9

Spring Appetizers, Snacks, & Salads

Artichokes Braised in White Wine

Ingredients

6 artichokes

2 tbsp olive oil

1 small onion, peeled and finely chopped

2 cloves garlic, peeled and finely sliced

1 cup white wine or dry sherry

salt

freshly grated nutmeg

Method

1 Remove the stalks and outer leaves from the artichokes and wash well. Cut each one into pieces. Heat the oil in a casserole and gently sauté the onion and garlic for about 4 minutes. Add the artichokes and wine, and season with salt and nutmeg. Cook gently until done (20–40 minutes, depending on size and type). Test by pulling a leaf; if done it will come away easily. If the liquid reduces too much you can add a little water.

Serves 4

Sweet Pepper Terrine with Basil Vinaigrette

Ingredients

butter for greasing

2 red and 2 yellow bell peppers, halved and deseeded

3 tbsp olive oil

1 red chili, deseeded and thinly sliced

8 oz/250 g tub ricotta

4 oz/125 g mature Cheddar, grated

1 tbsp Dijon mustard

1 tsp salt

3 medium eggs, beaten

Vinaigrette

2 tbsp white wine vinegar

2 tbsp extra virgin olive oil

4 tbsp sunflower oil

2 scallions, finely sliced

3 tbsp finely chopped fresh basil

salt and black pepper

Method

1 Preheat the oven to 375°F/190°C/Gas Mark 5. Butter a large piece of baking paper and line a 1 lb/455 g loaf tin, leaving enough paper to cover the top. Finely dice half the red and half the yellow pepper and set aside. Roughly chop the rest.

2 Heat the oil in a heavy-based saucepan, add the chopped peppers and chili, then cook, covered, for 20 minutes or until softened. Purée in a food processor or with a hand blender, then press through a sieve. Combine the ricotta, Cheddar, mustard, salt, and eggs, then stir in the purée and diced peppers. Pour into the tin, then fold the paper over to cover the terrine without touching. Place in a roasting tin.

3 Pour in enough boiling water to reach halfway up the sides of the loaf tin, then cook for 1 1/4 hours, adding more water if necessary. Cool for 2 hours, then place in the refrigerator for 1 hour. Invert onto a plate and peel off the paper. To make the vinaigrette, combine the ingredients, and mix well. Serve with the terrine.

Serves 4

Asian Gingered Coleslaw

Ingredients

1/4 **large curly cabbage, very finely sliced**

4 **baby bok choy, leaves separated and sliced**

8 **scallions, julienned lengthways**

7 **oz/200 g can sliced water chestnuts, drained**

2 **medium carrots, finely julienned**

2 **stalks lemon grass, very finely sliced**

4 **kaffir lime leaves, very finely sliced**

Dressing

2 **tbsp low-fat mayonnaise**

2 **tbsp low-fat yogurt**

juice of 2 lemons

juice of 1 lime

1 **tbsp freshly grated ginger**

4 **tbsp rice vinegar**

salt and pepper, to taste

Garnish

1 **bunch of cilantro, well washed and roughly chopped**

1/2 **cup toasted peanuts or sunflower seeds**

Method

1 Mix the cabbage in a large bowl with the sliced bok choy, scallions, water chestnuts, carrots, lemon grass, and lime leaves. Toss thoroughly.

2 In a jug, whisk together all the dressing ingredients until smooth and well seasoned, then pour over the salad ingredients and toss thoroughly until all the vegetables are coated with the dressing. To serve, mix through the cilantro at the last minute and sprinkle with the crushed peanuts or sunflower seeds.

Serves 4

Garlic Shrimps

Ingredients

2¹/₄ lb/1 kg shrimps

4 cloves garlic, crushed

1 small fresh chili, seeded and
   chopped

¹/₄ cup olive oil

juice of 2 lemons

black pepper

lemon wedges to garnish

Method

1   Place the shrimps in a shallow dish. If preferred shelled, remove the heads and shell, leaving the tails intact.

2   Combine the garlic, chili, oil, lemon juice, and pepper. Pour over the prawns and leave to stand for 20 minutes. Place the shrimps in a frying pan over medium heat and cook for about 3 minutes on each side, according to size, just until the shrimps turn red.

3   Place into individual serving dishes or onto a large platter. Pour the juices from the pan over the shrimps. Garnish with lemon and serve immediately.

Serves 4–6

Griddled Scallops with Orange Salsa

Ingredients

2 small oranges

4 sun-dried tomatoes in oil, drained and chopped

1 clove garlic, crushed

1 tbsp balsamic vinegar

4 tbsp extra virgin olive oil

salt and black pepper

1 large head fennel, cut lengthways into 8 slices

12 freshly prepared scallops

4 tbsp crème fraîche

arugula leaves to serve

Method

1 Slice the top and bottom off one of the oranges, then cut away the peel and pith, following the curve of the fruit. Cut between the membranes to release the segments, then chop roughly. Squeeze the juice of the other orange into a bowl, then add the chopped orange, tomatoes, garlic, vinegar, and 3 tablespoons of the oil, and season with salt and pepper.

2 Heat a ridged cast-iron griddle pan or heavy-based frying pan. Brush both sides of each fennel slice with half the remaining oil. Cook for 2–3 minutes on each side, until tender and charred. Transfer to serving plates and keep warm.

3 Brush the scallops with the remaining oil and cook for 1 minute, then turn and cook for 30 seconds or until cooked through. Top the fennel with 1 tablespoon of crème fraîche, 3 scallops, and the salsa. Serve with the arugua.

Serves 4

Potato Cakes with Smoked Salmon

Ingredients

11 oz/310 g floury potatoes such
  as King Edward, unpeeled

salt and black pepper

$^2/_3$ cup whole milk

1 large egg

1 oz/30 g all-purpose flour

4 scallions, finely sliced

1 tbsp oil

4 fl oz/115 mL crème fraîche

2 tbsp chopped fresh dill,
  plus extra to garnish

5 oz/145 g smoked salmon slices

lemon wedges to serve

Method

1 Cook the potatoes in boiling salted water for 15–20 minutes, until tender, then drain. Cool for a few minutes, then peel. Mash with the milk, season, then beat in the egg, flour, and scallions to make a batter.

2 Heat a heavy-based non-stick frying pan, then add a little of the oil. Make 4 potato cakes, using 2 tablespoons of batter for each. Fry for 2–3 minutes on each side until golden. Drain on paper towel and keep warm while you make 2 further batches of 4 potato cakes.

3 Mix together the crème fraîche and chopped dill. Serve the potato cakes topped with the salmon slices and a spoonful of the herby crème fraîche. Grind over some black pepper. Garnish with the extra dill and with lemon wedges.

Serves 4–6

Potted Chicken and Ham

Ingredients

7 oz/200 g butter

7 oz/200 g cooked skinless chicken
  or turkey, cut into pieces

3¹/₂ oz/100 g cooked ham,
  cut into pieces

black pepper

¹/₄ tsp ground nutmeg

pinch of ground allspice

pinch of cayenne pepper

4 fresh bay leaves

Method

1 To clarify the butter, place it in a small saucepan and melt over a low heat for 3–4 minutes, taking care not to let it brown. Line a sieve with damp muslin, place over a bow, and pour the butter into the sieve, discarding the milky deposit left in the pan. Leave the strained liquid (clarified butter) to cool for 5–10 minutes.

2 Meanwhile, blend the chicken or turkey, and the ham in a food processor until fairly smooth. Add the pepper, nutmeg, allspice, and cayenne to taste, and blend until combined. Gradually pour in just under three-quarters of the clarified butter, blending all the time until mixed.

3 Spoon the mixture into small dishes or ramekins and top each with a bay leaf. Pour over the remaining butter to seal, then refrigerate for 2–3 hours, or overnight.

Serves 4

Ricotta Herb Dip with Garlic Toasts

Ingredients

6 pitted green olives, finely chopped

1 tbsp chopped fresh tarragon

1 tbsp chopped fresh chives

1 tbsp chopped fresh mint

2 tsp finely grated lemon zest

8 oz/250 g tub ricotta cheese

black pepper

4 tbsp sun-dried tomato paste

1 large 5-cereal baguette, cut into
  ¹/₂ in/1 cm thick slices

1 clove garlic, halved

Method

1 Mix together the olives, tarragon, chives, mint, and lemon zest, then stir in the ricotta. Season with pepper and mix well.

2 Lightly stir the sun-dried tomato paste into the ricotta mixture to create a marbled effect, then spoon into a serving dish.

3 Preheat the broiler to high. Broil the baguette slices for 1–2 minutes on each side, until golden. Rub the cut surfaces of the garlic halves over the toast slices and serve them with the dip.

Serves 4

Deviled Whitebait

Ingredients

sunflower or groundnut oil
for deep-frying
5 tbsp all–purpose flour
salt and black pepper
$^1/_4$–$^1/_2$ tsp cayenne pepper
I tsp ground cilantro
14 oz/400 g frozen whitebait,
defrosted, rinsed, and dried
I oz/30 g parsley
lemon wedges to serve

Method

1 Heat the oil in a deep heavy-based saucepan. To check that the oil is hot enough for frying, drop in a cube of bread; it should turn brown and rise to the surface in 30 seconds.

2 Meanwhile, place the flour in a large plastic bag and add $^1/_2$ teaspoon of salt, black pepper, the cayenne pepper, and ground cilantro. Shake to mix, then add the whitebait to the bag a few at a time and shake gently to coat.

3 Fry the whitebait in batches for 4–5 minutes, until crisp and golden, then drain on paper towels. Fry the parsley for 30–45 seconds, taking care as the fat will spit, then drain on paper towels. Sprinkle the whitebait with salt and serve with the deep-fried parsley and the lemon wedges.

Serves 4

Plum Tomato, Lentil, and Basil Soup

Ingredients

3 oz/85 g continental lentils

2¹/₄ lb/1 kg plum tomatoes

1 tbsp olive oil

2 onions, chopped

2 tbsp sun-dried tomato paste

3 cups vegetable bouillon

1 bay leaf

black pepper

3 tbsp chopped fresh basil,
**   plus extra leaves to garnish**

Method

1 Rinse the lentils, drain, then add to a large saucepan of boiling water. Simmer, covered, for 25 minutes or until tender. Drain, rinse and set aside.

2 Meanwhile, place the tomatoes in a bowl, cover with boiling water, leave for 30 seconds, then drain. Remove the skins, deseed, and chop. Heat the oil in a large saucepan, add the onions, and cook for 10 minutes or until softened, stirring occasionally. Stir in the tomatoes, tomato paste, bouillon, bay leaf, and black pepper. Bring to the boil and simmer, covered, stirring occasionally, for 25 minutes or until all the vegetables are cooked.

3 Remove the pan from the heat and cool for a few minutes. Remove and discard the bay leaf, then purée the soup in a food processor until smooth. Return to a clean pan, stir in the lentils and chopped basil, then reheat gently. Serve garnished with fresh basil.

Serves 4

Thai Sour Shrimp Soup

Ingredients

2 stalks lemon grass

**11 oz/310 g whole raw
shrimps (shell on),
defrosted if frozen**

1 tbsp vegetable oil

4 cups chicken bouillon

1 clove garlic, crushed

**1 in/2¹/₂ cm piece fresh root ginger,
roughly chopped**

**grated zest of 1 lime and
juice of 2 limes**

**1 green chili, deseeded and
finely chopped**

salt and black pepper

1 tbsp fish sauce

**1 red chili, deseeded and sliced, and
2 tbsp chopped fresh cilantro
to garnish**

Method

1 Peel the outer layers from the lemon grass stalks and chop the lower white bulbous parts into 3 pieces, discarding the fibrous tops. Shell the shrimps, leaving the tails attached, and reserving the shells for the bouillon. Cut a slit along the back of each shrimp with a sharp knife and remove the thin black vein. Rinse the shrimps, then refrigerate until needed.

2 Heat the oil in a large saucepan. Fry the shrimp shell for 2–3 minutes, until pink. Add the bouillon, garlic, ginger, lemon grass, lime zest, green chili and salt to taste. Bring to the boil, then reduce the heat, cover, and simmer for 20 minutes.

3 Strain the bouillon and return to the pan. Stir in the fish sauce and lime juice, and bring to the boil. Add the shrimps, reduce the heat, and simmer for 3 minutes or until the shrimp turn pink and are cooked through. Season with pepper and serve garnished with red chili and cilantro.

Serves 4

Flaked Tuna Pasta in Tomato Dressing

Ingredients

8 oz/225 g dried whole-wheat pasta twists or shapes

4 scallions, sliced, plus thin strips to garnish

1 yellow bell pepper, deseeded and diced

4 oz/125 g sugar snap peas, chopped

7 oz/200 g can corn, drained

6 oz/170 g can tuna in water, drained and flaked

Dressing

5 tbsp tomato puree

1 tbsp extra virgin olive oil

2 tsp balsamic vinegar

pinch of superfine sugar

2 tbsp chopped fresh basil

black pepper

Method

1 Cook the pasta according to the instructions on the packet, until tender but firm to the bite. Drain, rinse under cold running water to cool, then drain thoroughly. Place in a serving bowl.

2 To make the dressing, whisk together the tomato purée, olive oil, vinegar, sugar, basil, and black pepper in a bowl until thoroughly mixed. Pour the dressing over the pasta, then toss to mix well.

3 Add the sliced scallions, yellow bell pepper, sugar snap peas, corn, and tuna to the pasta and toss lightly. Garnish with the scallion strips.

Serves 4

Marinated Chicken Salad with Warm Dressing

Ingredients

4 skinless boneless chicken breasts, cut into ¹/₂ in/1 cm strips

2 tbsp groundnut oil

2 tbsp sesame oil

2 cloves garlic, chopped

1–2 red or green chilies, deseeded and finely sliced

1 in/2¹/₂ cm piece fresh root ginger, finely grated

¹/₃ cup red wine vinegar

¹/₃ cup water

10 oz/285 g green salad leaves

Marinade

2 tbsp dark soy sauce

2 tbsp clear honey

1 tbsp sesame oil (optional)

Method

1 To make the marinade, mix together the soy sauce, honey, and sesame oil, if using. Place the chicken in a non-metallic bowl and pour the marinade over. Toss the chicken well to coat, then cover and refrigerate for 30 minutes.

2 Heat 1 tablespoon of the groundnut oil and 1 tablespoon of the sesame oil in a wok or large, heavy-based frying pan. Add the chicken and stir-fry for 5–6 minutes, until cooked through and browned. Remove from the pan and leave to cool.

3 Add the remaining oil, garlic, chili, and ginger to the pan and fry, stirring and scraping the bottom of the pan, for 3–4 minutes, until the garlic starts to brown. Stir in the vinegar and water, bring to the boil, then remove from the heat.

4 Arrange the salad leaves on plates, top with the chicken strips, and spoon the warm dressing over.

Serves 4

Celery Root and Herb Remoulade

Ingredients

2 medium eggs

1 lb/500 g celery root, grated

2 tbsp olive oil

1 tbsp sesame oil

juice of 1 lemon

3 tbsp chopped fresh parsley

3 tbsp snipped fresh chives

salt and black pepper

Method

1 Bring a saucepan of water to the boil. Add the eggs and boil for 10 minutes. Cool under cold running water, then remove the shells and finely chop the eggs.

2 Place the celery root and chopped eggs in a large bowl. Mix together the olive oil, sesame oil, and lemon juice and pour over the celery root and eggs. Add the parsley, chives, and seasoning, then mix thoroughly.

Serves 4–6

Spring Mains

Broiled Salmon Steaks with Mint Vinaigrette

Ingredients

4 salmon steaks, about
   6 oz/170 g each
salt and black pepper

Vinaigrette
2 tbsp chopped fresh mint,
   plus extra leaves to garnish
1 small green onion, finely chopped
6 tbsp olive or vegetable oil
juice of 1 lemon

Method

1 Preheat the broiler to high and line the broiler tray with kitchen foil. Place the salmon steaks on top and season lightly. Broil for 4–5 minutes on each side, until lightly browned and cooked through.

2 Meanwhile, make the vinaigrette. Mix together the mint, green onion, oil, and lemon juice, then season to taste. Spoon over the salmon steaks and garnish with mint.

Serves 4

Baked Lamb Chops with Tomatoes and Peppers

Ingredients

6 large lamb loin chops, trimmed of excess fat

chopped fresh parsley to garnish

Marinade

3 tbsp chopped fresh thyme or 2 tsp dried thyme

3 tbsp olive oil

3 tbsp red wine vinegar

salt and black pepper

Topping

1 lb/500 g plum tomatoes

1 large green bell pepper, deseeded and finely chopped

1 red onion, finely chopped

2 large cloves garlic, finely chopped

Method

1 To make the marinade, place the thyme, oil, vinegar, and seasoning in a non-metallic ovenproof dish. Add the chops and turn to coat. Cover and place in the refrigerator for 1 hour.

2 Preheat the oven to 425°F/220°C/Gas Mark 7. Place the tomatoes in a bowl and cover with boiling water. Leave for 30 seconds, then peel, deseed, and chop.

3 Mix together the tomatoes, green pepper, onion, and garlic, then season well. Spoon the mixture over the chops. Bake for 35 minutes for medium-cooked chops, or 45 minutes for chops that are well done. Cover with foil and set aside for 5 minutes to rest. Garnish with parsley.

Serves 6

Lemon Chicken Stir-Fry

Ingredients

finely grated zest and juice of 1 lemon

2 cloves garlic, crushed

2 tbsp chopped fresh cilantro

black pepper

12 oz/340 g skinless boneless chicken breasts, cut into strips

2 tbsp sesame seeds

1 tbsp sesame oil

1 in/2^1/$_2$ cm piece fresh root ginger, finely chopped

2 carrots, cut into matchsticks

1 leek, thinly sliced

6 oz/170 g snow peas

4 oz/125 g bean sprouts

1 tbsp dry sherry

1 tbsp light soy sauce

Method

1 In a non-metallic bowl, mix the lemon zest and juice, half of the garlic, and the cilantro. Season with black pepper and add the chicken. Turn to coat, then cover and refrigerate for 1 hour.

2 Heat a non-stick wok or large frying pan and dry-fry the sesame seeds for 30 seconds, stirring. Remove and set aside. Add the oil to the wok or pan, heat, then stir-fry the ginger and remaining garlic for 30 seconds. Add the chicken and marinade and stir-fry for 4 minutes.

3 Add the carrots and leek and stir-fry for 1–2 minutes. Add the snow peas and bean sprouts and stir-fry for 2–3 minutes, until everything is tender. Pour in the sherry and soy sauce, and sizzle for 1–2 minutes, then sprinkle with the sesame seeds.

Serves 4

Fish Cakes with Tartare Sauce

Ingredients

1 lb/500 g potatoes, cut into chunks

salt and black pepper

1 lb/500 g cod fillets

7 fl oz/200 mL whole milk

2 tbsp chopped fresh parsley

4 scallions, finely sliced

4 tbsp all-purpose flour

2 medium eggs, beaten

3 oz/80 g dried breadcrumbs

oil for shallow frying

Tartare Sauce

6 tbsp mayonnaise

2 tbsp crème fraîche

1 tbsp capers, rinsed, dried,
   and chopped

2 tbsp finely chopped
   pickles

1 tbsp chopped fresh parsley

1 tbsp chopped fresh tarragon

$1/2$ tsp finely grated lemon zest

Method

1 Cook the potatoes in boiling salted water for 15 minutes or until tender. Drain, then mash and leave to cool. Meanwhile, place the fish in a frying pan and pour in the milk. Cook over a low heat, partly covered, for 10 minutes or until just cooked. Remove the fish from the milk and flake, discarding any skin or bones.

2 Mix together the fish, mash, parsley, and scallions and season well. Shape into 8 cakes, 2 cm/$3/4$ in thick. Season the flour with salt and pepper. Dip the fish cakes into the seasoned flour, then the beaten egg, and finally the breadcrumbs, coating well. Refrigerate for 1 hour.

3 To make the tartare sauce, mix the mayonnaise with the crème fraîche, capers, pickles, herbs, lemon zest and pepper.

4 Heat $1/4$ in/5 mm oil in a frying pan and fry half the fish cakes for 5–6 minutes on each side, until golden. Drain on kitchen towels, then keep warm while you cook the rest. Serve with the tartare sauce.

Serves 4

Crusted Salmon with Orange and Fennel Salad

Ingredients

1 oz/30 g butter, plus
    extra for greasing
1 tbsp olive oil
1 onion, chopped
1 in/2¹/₂ cm piece fresh
    root ginger, chopped
8 anchovy fillets, drained
    and chopped
5 tbsp ground almonds
3 tbsp medium matzo meal
    or fresh breadcrumbs
2 tbsp chopped fresh dill,
    plus extra to garnish
black pepper
6 salmon steaks, about
    7 oz/200 g each

Salad
2 oranges
2 bulbs fennel, finely chopped
1 large red onion, finely chopped
juice of 1 lemon
3 tbsp extra virgin olive oil
salt and black pepper

Method

1 To make the salad, slice the top and bottom off each orange with a sharp knife, then cut off the peel and pith, following the curve of the fruit. Cut out the segments, leaving the membranes behind, and chop. Mix with the fennel, onion, lemon juice, oil, and seasoning, then cover and refrigerate for 30 minutes. Preheat the oven to 400°F/200°C/Gas Mark 6. Grease an ovenproof dish.

2 In a small, heavy-based pan, heat the butter and oil, then add the onion and ginger, and fry, stirring occasionally, for 10 minutes to soften the onion. Add the anchovies and cook for 2 minutes or until they break down. Purée the mixture in a food processor or use a hand blender, then mix in the almonds, matzo meal or breadcrumbs, dill and pepper.

3 Place the salmon steaks in the ovenproof dish and spread the anchovy mixture over the top, pressing down well. Cook for 10 minutes, then increase the heat to 450°F/230°C/Gas Mark 8. Cook for a further 8–10 minutes, until the salmon is tender and cooked through and the topping has browned. Serve with the salad, garnished with dill.

Serves 6

Thai-Spiced Chicken with Zucchinis

Ingredients

1 tbsp olive oil

1 clove garlic, finely chopped

1 in/2^1/$_2$ cm fresh root ginger, finely chopped

1 small fresh red chili, deseeded and finely chopped

12 oz/340 g skinless boneless chicken breasts, cut into strips

1 tbsp Thai 7-spice seasoning

1 red and 1 yellow bell pepper, deseeded and sliced

2 zucchinis, thinly sliced

7 oz/200 g can bamboo shoots, drained

2 tbsp dry sherry or apple juice

1 tbsp light soy sauce

black pepper

2 tbsp chopped fresh cilantro, plus extra to garnish

Method

1 Heat the oil in a non-stick wok or large frying pan. Add the garlic, ginger, and chili and stir-fry for 30 seconds to release the flavors.

2 Add the chicken and Thai seasoning and stir-fry for 4 minutes or until the chicken has colored. Add the peppers and zucchinis and stir-fry for 1–2 minutes, until slightly softened.

3 Stir in the bamboo shoots and stir-fry for another 2–3 minutes, until the chicken is cooked through and tender. Add the sherry or apple juice, soy sauce, and black pepper, and sizzle for 1–2 minutes. Remove from the heat and stir in the chopped fresh cilantro. Serve garnished with the extra cilantro.

Serves 4

Pasta Primavera

Ingredients

2 oz/55 g butter

¹/₂ lb/250 g baby spinach

**1 lb/500 g fresh peas
(unshelled weight), shelled**

**1 lb/500 g fava beans
(unshelled weight), shelled**

salt and black pepper

4 tbsp crème fraîche

1 bunch scallions, finely sliced

**2 tbsp finely chopped
fresh parsley**

3 oz/85 g Parmesan cheese, grated

**12 oz/340 g dried penne
(pasta quills)**

Method

1 Melt the butter in a saucepan, add the spinach, cover, and cook for 5 minutes or until the leaves wilt. Set aside to cool. Cook the peas and beans in a little boiling salted water for 5 minutes or until tender, then drain.

2 Blend the spinach and crème fraîche to a purée in a food processor or use a hand blender. Return the purée to the pan and stir in the peas and beans. Mix in the scallions and parsley, season, and add half the Parmesan. Keep warm over a low heat.

3 Meanwhile, cook the pasta in boiling salted water according to the packet instructions, until tender but still firm to the bite. Drain, then toss with the spinach sauce. Serve with the remaining Parmesan.

Serves 4

Roasted Vegetable and Broccoli Couscous

Ingredients

4 parsnips, cut into chunks

salt

2 sweet potatoes, cut into chunks

4 turnips, quartered

2 cloves garlic, crushed

5 tbsp olive oil

4 tbsp apple or redcurrant jelly

11 oz/310 g couscous

1 lb/500 g tomatoes, chopped

**handful each of chopped fresh
  parsley, chives, and basil**

juice of 1 lemon

**11 oz/310 g broccoli,
  cut into florets**

Method

1 Preheat the oven to 400°F/200°C/Gas Mark 6.
Cook the parsnips in a saucepan of boiling salted
water for 2 minutes, then drain. Place in a roasting
tin with the sweet potatoes, turnips, garlic, and 3
tablespoons of oil, turning to coat. Sprinkle with salt,
then cook for 30 minutes or until lightly browned.

2 Melt the apple or redcurrant jelly in a pan with
4 tablespoons of water for 2–3 minutes, until it
turns syrupy. Turn the vegetables in the tin and
carefully spoon the syrup over. Return to the oven
for 10 minutes or until browned and glossy.

3 Meanwhile, prepare the couscous according to
the packet instructions. Heat the rest of the oil in a
frying pan and cook the tomatoes for 2–3 minutes,
until softened. Add the couscous and heat through,
then mix in the herbs and lemon juice. Meanwhile,
boil the broccoli florets for 2 minutes or until
tender, then drain. Serve the couscous with the
roasted vegetables and broccoli arranged on top.

Serves 4

Roast Chicken with Basil and Red Onion

Ingredients

3 lb/1¹/₂ kg chicken

¹/₂ oz/15 g fresh basil

6 tbsp extra virgin olive oil

juice of ¹/₂ lemon

sea salt and freshly ground

  black pepper

onions

4 medium red onions

grated zest of ¹/₂ lemon

1 clove garlic, crushed

Method

1 Preheat the oven to 350°F/180°C/Gas Mark 4. Place the chicken in a roasting tray. Gently work the skin away from the flesh with your fingers and tuck 6–7 basil leaves under the breast skin of the chicken. Place the remaining basil in a liquidizer with the olive oil, lemon juice, and seasoning, and blend until smooth. Brush the chicken with half the basil oil and cook for 40 minutes.

2 Meanwhile, prepare the onions. Peel them and slice off the root bottom to give a flat base. Make 4 cuts, in a criss-cross shape, across the top of each onion, coming only halfway down, so the onions open slightly. Combine the lemon zest with the garlic and sprinkle this over the onions.

3 Add the onions to the chicken in the tray and brush well with some of the basil oil. Brush the remaining oil over the chicken and cook for a further 40 minutes or until cooked through. Cover and allow the chicken to rest for 10 minutes before carving.

Serves 4

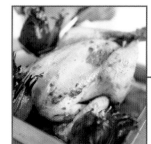

Spring Baking

Fresh Strawberry Scones

Ingredients

8 oz/225 g whole-wheat flour

2 teaspoons baking powder

pinch of salt

2 oz/55 g margarine or butter

1 oz/30 g superfine sugar

3 oz/85 g fresh strawberries, chopped

**$^1/_4$ cup low-fat milk, plus extra
   for glazing**

Method

1 Preheat the oven to 400°F/200°C/Gas Mark 6. Put the flour, baking powder, and salt in a large bowl and stir to mix. Lightly rub in the margarine or butter until the mixture resembles breadcrumbs.

2 Mix in the sugar and strawberries, then add enough milk to form a soft dough. Turn the dough out onto a floured surface, knead lightly, then carefully roll to a thickness of $^3/_4$ in/2 cm.

3 Cut out 12 rounds, using a 2 in/5 cm pastry cutter, and place on a baking sheet. Brush with milk to glaze. Bake for 8–10 minutes, until well risen and golden brown. Transfer to a wire rack to cool.

Makes 12 scones

Greek Walnut Syrup Cake

Ingredients

2 lb/500 g plain yogurt

**4¼ oz/125 g soft butter, plus extra
  for greasing**

3 tbsp pistachio kernels, ground

¾ cup sugar

zest of 1 orange

2 large eggs

2 cups all-purpose flour

1 tsp baking powder

1 cup dried apricots, chopped

1 cup pistachio kernels, chopped

½ cup slivered almonds, toasted

½ cup honey

zest of 2 oranges

1 cup orange juice

2 fl oz/55 mL water

10 mint leaves, torn

Method

1 The day before baking, line a large sieve with muslin and spoon the yogurt into the sieve. Place the sieve over a bowl and cover with plastic wrap. Allow this to sit undisturbed in the refrigerator for 12 hours. Discard the liquid and set the yogurt aside.

2 On the day of baking, preheat the oven to 350°F/180°C/Gas Mark 4. Generously grease a 11 in/28 cm or 10 in/26 cm springform cake tin and sprinkle the ground pistachio nuts around the tin. Tip the tin to help the nuts adhere to the greased sides.

3 Beat the butter, sugar and orange zest together until thick and pale, then add the eggs, one at a time, and beat well after each addition. Add the yogurt and continue to beat on a slow speed until the batter is well mixed.

4 In a separate bowl, mix together the flour and baking powder, and sift into the cake batter. Mix gently but thoroughly and finally add the chopped apricots and nuts, and mix to distribute.

5 Pour the cake batter into the prepared tin and bake for 50 minutes or until 'springy' when pressed gently in the centre. Meanwhile, simmer together the honey, orange zest, orange juice, water and torn mint leaves for 6 minutes. Strain and set aside.

6 When the cake has finished baking, remove it from the oven and place on a tray or piece of foil to catch any drips. Pour the orange syrup over the cake and allow to cool. Serve with a little yogurt that has been flavoured with some honey and cinnamon to taste, and orange segments if desired.

Serves 6

Spiced Apple Muffins

Ingredients

7 oz/200 g whole-wheat flour

I tsp baking powder

I tsp ground mixed spice

pinch of salt

2 oz/55 g light soft brown sugar

I medium egg, beaten

7 fl oz/200 mL low-fat milk

2 oz/55 g margarine or butter, melted

**I cooking apple, peeled,
cored, and chopped**

Method

1 Preheat the oven to 400°F/200°C/Gas Mark 6. Line a muffin or deep bun tin with 9 muffin cases and set aside. Place the flour, baking powder, mixed spice, and salt in a bowl and mix well.

2 In a separate large bowl, mix together the sugar, egg, milk, and margarine or butter, then gently fold in the flour mixture – just enough to combine them. The mixture should look quite lumpy; it will produce heavy muffins if overmixed. Gently fold in the apple.

3 Divide the mixture among the muffin cases. Bake in the oven for 20 minutes or until risen and golden brown. Transfer to a wire rack to cool.

Serves 9

Hot Brownies with White Chocolate Sauce

Ingredients

**3 oz/85 g soft margarine or butter,
plus extra for greasing**

3 oz/85 g soft dark brown sugar

1 large egg, beaten

1 tbsp corn syrup

1 tbsp cocoa powder, sifted

2 oz/55 g whole-wheat flour, sifted

**1 oz/30 g pecan nuts or
walnuts, chopped**

White Chocolate Sauce

1 tablespoon cornstarch

7 fl oz/200 mL whole milk

**2 oz/55 g white chocolate, broken
into small chunks**

Method

1 Preheat the oven to 350°F/180°C/Gas Mark 4.
Grease the sides and base of an 7 in/18 cm square
cake tin. Beat the margarine or butter and sugar in
a bowl until pale and creamy, then beat in the egg,
corn syrup, cocoa powder, and flour until it forms a
thick, smooth batter. Stir in the nuts.

2 Spoon the mixture into the tin, smooth the top,
and bake for 35–40 minutes, until well risen and just
firm to the touch.

3 Meanwhile, make the chocolate sauce. Blend the
cornstarch with 1 tablespoon of the milk. Heat the
rest of the milk in a saucepan, add the cornstarch
mixture, then gently bring to the boil, stirring as the
sauce thickens. Cook gently for 1–2 minutes.

4 Add the white chocolate, then remove from the
heat and stir until it melts. Cut the brownies into 8
pieces and serve warm with the chocolate sauce.

Serves 4

Sticky Chocolate and Raspberry Slice

Ingredients

3 oz/85 g sweet butter,
   plus extra for greasing
3 oz/85 g semi-sweet chocolate,
   broken into chunks
3 oz/85 g fresh or frozen raspberries,
   defrosted if frozen, plus extra to
   decorate
2 medium eggs, separated
1/4 cup superfine sugar
1 oz/30 g ground almonds
1 oz/30 g cocoa powder, sifted
1 oz/30 g all-purpose flour, sifted
confectioners sugar to dust, and
   fresh mint to decorate

Raspberry Sauce
5 oz/145 g fresh or frozen raspberries,
   defrosted if frozen
1 tbsp superfine sugar

Method

1 Preheat the oven to 350°F/180°C/Gas Mark 4. Grease the base and sides of an 7 in/18 cm loose-bottomed cake tin and line with baking paper. Melt the butter and chocolate in a bowl set over a saucepan of simmering water, stirring frequently. Cool slightly.

2 Meanwhile, press the raspberries through a sieve. Whisk the egg yolks and superfine sugar until pale and creamy, then mix in the almonds, cocoa, flour, melted chocolate, and sieved raspberries.

3 Whisk the egg whites until they form stiff peaks (this is best done with an electric whisk). Fold a little into the chocolate mixture to loosen, then fold in the remainder. Spoon into the tin and cook for 25 minutes or until risen and just firm. Cool for 1 hour.

4 To make the raspberry sauce, push the raspberries through a sieve, then stir in the sugar, if using. Remove the cake from the tin and dust with the confectioners' sugar. Serve the slice with the sauce, decorated with mint and raspberries.

Serves 8

Strawberry Trifle Brûlée

Ingredients

3 oz/85 g amaretti cookies, roughly crushed, or 2 trifle sponges, halved

3 tbsp madeira, sweet sherry or kirsch

3 fl oz/85 mL whipping or heavy cream

3 fl oz/85 mL ready-made custard

3 oz/85 g strawberries, hulled and halved

3 tbsp raw sugar

Method

1 Divide the cookies or sponge halves among 4 x $^1/_4$ pint/150 mL ramekins and spoon over the madeira, sherry, or kirsch.

2 Whip the cream until it forms soft peaks, then fold in the custard and strawberries. Divide the cream mixture among the ramekins. Smooth the tops and sprinkle over a thick layer of sugar.

3 Meanwhile, preheat the broiler to high. Place the ramekins under the broiler for 2–3 minutes, until the sugar caramelizes. Leave to cool, then refrigerate for 2 hours before serving.

Serves 4

Sweet Spring

Creamy Raspberry Fool

Ingredients

11 oz/310 g fresh raspberries

2 oz/55 g superfine sugar

7 fl oz/200 mL carton crème fraîche

Method

1 Reserve a few raspberries for decoration, then mix the rest with half of the sugar and press the mixture through a sieve. Stir in the remaining sugar to taste.

2 Place the crème fraîche in a large bowl and gently fold in the raspberry purée until combined. Spoon into small coffee cups or glasses and refrigerate for 2–3 hours to firm up slightly. Serve decorated with the reserved raspberries.

Serves 4

Cheat's Key Lime Pie

Ingredients

3 fl oz/85 mL whipping or
  heavy cream
²/₃ cup condensed milk
grated zest and juice of 2 limes
7 in/18 cm sweet pastry case
10 oz/285 g pack meringue mix

Method

1 Whip the cream until it forms soft peaks. Gently fold in the condensed milk, lime zest, and juice. Spoon the mixture into the pastry case and place in the refrigerator for 1 hour – the mixture is quite loose at first but firms up when refrigerated.

2 Meanwhile, make the meringue topping according to the packet instructions, whisking until it forms stiff peaks (this is best done with an electric whisk).

3 Preheat the broiler to medium. Spoon the meringue over the cream mixture. Broil for 2–4 minutes, until the meringue turns golden. Serve either warm or cold.

Serves 6

Hazelnut Meringues with Raspberry Sherbet

Ingredients

10 oz/285 g pack meringue mix

2 oz/55 g roasted chopped hazelnuts

2 tsp cornstarch

7 fl oz/200 mL carton crème fraîche

3¹/₂ oz/100 g fresh raspberries

fresh mint to decorate

Sorbet

**9 oz/255 g fresh or frozen raspberries,
   defrosted if frozen**

1 ripe banana, mashed

juice of 1 orange

Method

1 First make the sherbet. Beat the raspberries with the banana and orange juice, until thoroughly combined. Transfer to a freezer container and freeze for 2–3 hours, stirring once or twice.

2 Preheat the oven to 300°F/300°F/Gas Mark 2. Line 2 baking sheets with baking paper. Prepare the meringue mix according to the packet instructions, whisking until it forms stiff peaks (this is best done with an electric whisk).

3 Fold in the hazelnuts and cornstarch. Spoon the mixture onto the baking sheets, making 3 circles on each. Swirl the tops with a fork to flatten, then cook for 1 hour or until crisp. Cool for 20 minutes.

4 Top the meringues with the crème fraîche. Place small balls or curls of the sherbet on top along with the raspberries, and decorate with the fresh mint.

Serves 6

Glazed Apples in Brandy Snap Baskets

Ingredients

2 large eating apples, peeled, cored, and thickly sliced

1 oz/30 g butter

1 tbsp superfine sugar

2 tbsp brandy or calvados (optional)

2 tbsp lemon curd

$^1/_2$ cup crème fraîche

6 brandy-snap baskets

thin strips lemon zest, pared with a vegetable peeler, to decorate

Method

1 Place the apples in a saucepan with the butter, sugar, and brandy or calvados, if using. Simmer for 5 minutes or until the apples have softened.

2 Mix together the lemon curd and crème fraîche, then divide among the brandy snap baskets. Spoon the apple mixture over, decorate with the lemon zest, and serve immediately.

Serves 6

Honeyed Figs with Mascarpone

Ingredients

**12–16 fresh figs, depending
  on their size**
2 tbsp clear honey
1 tbsp pine nut
3¹/₂ oz/100 g mascarpone

Method

1 Preheat the oven to 350°F/180°C/Gas Mark 4. Cut a deep cross into each fig at the stalk end, then open out slightly. Place the figs close together in an ovenproof dish to keep them upright.

2 Drizzle the honey over and inside the figs, then cook for 10 minutes or until soft. Meanwhile, place a frying pan over a medium heat and dry-fry the pine nuts for 2 minutes or until golden, stirring often.

3 Transfer 3–4 figs to each serving plate, scatter the pine nuts around them, and serve with a spoonful of mascarpone.

Serves 4

It's party time! The long sunny days and warm evenings of summer are perfect for entertaining friends and family. Some of the wonderful seasonal ingredients available in summer include avocados, basil, blueberries, cherries, eggplant, green beans, peaches, summer squash, tomatoes, and watermelon. Our summer section includes recipes for party food such as Vine Tomatoes and Goat's Cheese Bruschetta; light soups; fresh crispy salads, such as Smoked Mackerel, Orange, and Lentil Salad; quick stir-fries; and refreshing fruity desserts, including Raspberry and Elderflower Fool. There are also plenty of recipes for barbecue fare, including a great recipe for paella.

Summer

Summer Appetizers, Snacks, & Salads

Breadsticks Wrapped in Proscuitto and Arugula

Ingredients

¹/₂ oz/15 g arugula or basil leaves

3 tbsp olive oil

6 thin slices prosciutto

6 breadsticks

Method

1 Brush the arugula or basil leaves with a little of the oil. Put a few in the middle of each prosciutto slice, then place a breadstick in the center, leaving about 3 in/7¹/₂ cm uncovered to use as a handle.

2 Tightly wrap the ham around the breadstick, tucking it in neatly at the top. Brush the prosciutto with the rest of the oil.

Serves 6

Tricolore Canapés

Ingredients

Cucumber Bowls

1 cucumber

3¹/₂ oz/100 g soft cheese

1 tbsp chopped fresh tarragon

salt and black pepper

Tomato Toasts

3 slices thick-cut sandwich loaf

1 clove garlic, crushed

3 tbsp olive oil

2 tbsp pesto

5¹/₂ oz/155 g mozzarella ball,
   cut into 12 slices

3 small tomatoes, thinly sliced
   and ends discarded

12 small pitted black olives

Salmon Rounds

4 slices dark or light rye bread

¹/₂ oz/15 g butter, softened

5 oz/145 g smoked salmon,
   cut into ribbons

2 tsp lemon juice

3 tbsp ricotta or cream cheese

1 tsp horseradish cream

Method

1 Place the sandwich and rye bread slices for the tomato toasts and salmon rounds in the refrigerator for 2 hours to chill thoroughly.

2 Make the cucumber bowls. Peel strips from the length of the cucumber to give a striped effect. Cut it into ¹/₂ in/1 cm thick rounds, then, using a tespoon, remove some of the seeds from each round to make a hollow. Pat dry with paper towels. Mix the soft cheese with the tarragon and season. Fill the hollows with the soft cheese mixture, season with black pepper and refrigerate for 1 hour.

3 For the tomato toasts, preheat the oven to 400°F/200°C/Gas Mark 6. Using a 2 in/5 cm pastry cutter, stamp 4 rounds from each slice of the chilled sandwich bread. Mix together the garlic and oil. Brush a baking tray with half the garlic oil, put the rounds on it, and brush with the rest of the oil. Cook for 10 minutes or until golden. Cool, then spread with the pesto and top with the mozzarella, tomatoes, and olives. Season with pepper.

4 Make the salmon rounds. Stamp 3 rounds from each slice of the chilled rye bread, using the pastry cutter, and butter them. Mix together the salmon, lemon juice, horseradish, ricotta or cream cheese and seasoning. Spoon onto the rounds.

Serves 6

Vine Tomatoes and Goat's Cheese Bruschetta

Ingredients

1 lb/455 g small vine-ripened tomatoes

2 tbsp extra virgin olive oil

1 clove garlic, crushed

4 sprigs fresh thyme

**4 thick slices ciabatta, cut
  on the diagonal**

4 tbsp ready-made tapenade

**3 1/2 oz/100 g soft goat's cheese,
  cut into chunks**

fresh basil leaves to garnish

Method

1 Preheat the oven to 425°F/220°C/Gas Mark 7. Place the tomatoes, still on the vine, in a roasting tin and drizzle the oil over. Scatter with the garlic and thyme sprigs. Roast for 15 minutes or until the tomatoes are tender. Divide the tomatoes into 4 portions of roughly the same size, each still attached to part of the vine.

2 Meanwhile, preheat the broiler to high. Toast the bread on both sides until golden. Spread each slice with 1 tablespoon of tapenade, add a few chunks of goat's cheese, and top with the tomatoes on the vine. Drizzle with the juices from the roasting tin and sprinkle with the basil leaves.

Serves 4

Spicy Chicken Wings with Orange

Ingredients

12 chicken wings

**10 oz/285 g bottle hoi sin sauce
or barbecue sauce**

3 oranges

4^1/$_2$ oz/125 g green salad leaves

3 scallions, sliced

Method

1 Place the chicken wings in a shallow non-metallic dish and pour the sauce over. Squeeze the juice from 1 orange and pour into the empty sauce bottle. Give it a shake to release all the sauce, then pour the juice over the chicken. Turn the chicken to coat well, cover, and place in the refrigerator to marinate for 10 minutes.

2 Preheat the broiler to high. Place the chicken wings in a single layer on a large baking tray and pour the marinade over, reserving a little for basting. Broil the wings for 20 minutes, turning frequently, and basting with the reserved marinade, until the flesh is cooked through and the skin is charred.

3 Meanwhile, peel the remaining oranges and divide into segments. Divide the salad leaves among 4 plates, add the orange segments and scallions and top with the hot chicken wings.

Serves 4

Smoked Trout Rillettes

Ingredients

2 x 4¹/₂ oz/125 g packs smoked trout fillets

finely grated zest and juice of 1 lemon

2 tbsp dry sherry

1¹/₂ oz/45 g butter, softened, plus 1¹/₂ oz/45 g butter, melted, for sealing (optional)

1 tsp capers, drained and chopped, plus extra to garnish (optional)

fresh herbs to garnish (optional)

Method

1 Flake the fish into a bowl and combine with the lemon zest and juice, sherry, softened butter, and capers. Alternatively, blend the ingredients in a food processor or use a hand blender.

2 Spoon the mixture into small bowls or ramekins. Pour the melted butter over, if using, and garnish with the herbs or capers, if using. Cover and place in the refrigerator for 30 minutes or until the butter has set.

Serves 4

Smoked Salmon Summer Platter

Ingredients

10 oz/285 g small new potatoes

salt and black pepper

24 thin asparagus spears

**1 tbsp chopped fresh dill,
  plus extra to garnish**

$^1/_2$ cup crème fraîche

**6 oz/170 g smoked salmon,
  thinly sliced**

Method

1 Cook the potatoes in boiling salted water for 15 minutes or until tender, then drain well.

2 Meanwhile, cut the coarse ends off the asparagus spears. Cook the asparagus in boiling salted water for 3–4 minutes, until just tender. Drain well.

3 Stir the chopped dill into the crème fraîche, then season to taste. Arrange the asparagus and potatoes on plates, then top with the salmon slices. Grind over a little pepper and garnish with dill. Serve with the herby crème fraîche.

Serves 4

Spinach and Goat's Cheese Pita Pizzas

Ingredients

4 oz/115 g sun-dried tomatoes in oil, drained, plus 2 tbsp oil from the jar

2 tbsp tomato paste

1 clove garlic, roughly chopped

2 tsp finely chopped fresh thyme or $^1/_2$ tsp dried thyme

$^1/_2$ lb/225 g baby spinach

6 mini pita breads

6 cherry tomatoes, quartered

$3^1/_2$ oz/100 g soft goat's cheese, sliced

1 tbsp sesame seeds

Method

1 Preheat the oven to 450°F/230°C/Gas Mark 8. Blend the sun-dried tomatoes, tomato paste and garlic to a purée in a food processor or using a hand blender. Mix in the thyme.

2 Bring a saucepan of water to the boil, immerse the spinach, remove, and refresh in a bowl of cold water. Drain, then drizzle the sun-dried tomato oil over the top.

3 Spread the tomato and garlic purée over the pita breads and top with the spinach. Scatter over the cherry tomatoes, cheese, and sesame seeds. Cook for 10 minutes or until the cheese has melted slightly and started to brown.

Serves 4

Shrimp and Avocado Cocktail

Ingredients

14 oz/400 g cooked peeled shrimps, defrosted if frozen

8 tbsp mayonnaise

4 tbsp tomato ketchup

2 sticks celery, finely chopped

1 scallions, finely sliced, or

1 tbsp finely chopped onion

salt and black pepper

2 avocados

squeeze of lemon juice

Method

1 Mix together the shrimps, mayonnaise, and tomato ketchup in a bowl, then stir in the celery and scallions, and season to taste.

2 Halve the avocados, remove the stones, and peel. Dice the flesh, then toss in the lemon juice to stop it browning. Add to the shrimp mixture, stirring lightly, then transfer to glasses or serving plates and grind a little pepper over the top.

Serves 4

Roasted Pepper and Tomato Soup

Ingredients

3 red or orange bell peppers, halved
   and deseeded
1 onion, unpeeled and halved
4 large plum tomatoes
4 cloves garlic, unpeeled
1 1/2 cups chicken
   or vegetable bouillon
1 tbsp tomato paste
salt and black pepper
2 tbsp chopped fresh parsley

Method

1 Preheat the oven to 400°F/200°C/Gas Mark 6. Place the peppers and onion on a baking sheet, cut-side down, and add the whole tomatoes and garlic. Cook in the oven for 30 minutes or until tender and well browned.

2 Leave the vegetables and garlic to cool for 10 minutes, then peel them. Place the vegetables and garlic in a food processor with half the bouillon, and blend until smooth.

3 Return to the pan, add the remaining bouillon and tomato paste, then bring to the boil. Season to taste and scatter the parsley over just before serving.

Serves 4

Lettuce, Avocado and Peanut Salad

Ingredients

2 Bibb lettuces, leaves separated

1 head Belgian endive, leaves separated

2 small ripe avocados, stoned, peeled, and cut into chunks

3 scallions, chopped

3 tbsp salted peanuts

Dressing

1 tbsp lemon juice

1 clove garlic, crushed

3 tbsp olive oil

2 tbsp smooth peanut butter

salt and black pepper

Method

1 To make the dressing, put the lemon juice, garlic, oil, and peanut butter into a bowl, combine thoroughly and season.

2 Arrange the lettuce leaves, endive, and avocado in a large shallow dish. Pour the dressing over and sprinkle with the scallions and peanuts.

Serves 4

Fish Noodle Soup

Ingredients

1 lb/500 g white fish fillets

vegetable oil

3 oz/85 g scallions

1 tsp chopped, fresh ginger

1 tsp garlic, chopped or crushed

**1 red bell pepper, seeded
and chopped**

4 cups fish bouillon or water

1 tbsp oyster sauce

$^1/_2$ tsp ground black pepper

1 tsp sesame oil

1 tbsp dry sherry

8 oz/225 g egg noodles, boiled

1 tsp sesame oil, extra

**$^1/_2$ red bell pepper, extra seeded
and chopped for garnish**

Method

1 Chop fish into bite-sized pieces. Heat enough vegetable oil to deep-fry the fish for 2$^1/_2$ minutes. Remove and drain. Cut the scallions into 1$^1/_2$ in/4 cm sections, separating the white parts from the green.

2 Heat 3 tablespoons of oil and brown the ginger and soften the garlic. Add the fish, bell pepper, and white sections of the scallions. Stir-fry for 3 minutes, then add the bouillon or water and boil. Add the green scallions sections, oyster sauce, black pepper, oil, and sherry, and simmer for 1 minute, stirring.

3 Add the hot, cooked, drained noodles and extra 1 teaspoon of oil. Stir through until hot. Serve immediately, garnished with the chopped red pepper.

Serves 4

Tomato and Bread Salad with Pesto Dressing

Ingredients

I French bread baton, cubed

2 tbsp olive oil

3 large tomatoes, cut into
I in/2^{1}/$_{2}$ cm chunks

I small red onion, thinly sliced

3^{1}/$_{2}$ oz/100 g feta, crumbled

handful of fresh basil leaves, torn

Dressing

3 tbsp olive oil

I red chili, deseeded and
finely chopped

2 tbsp red pesto

2 tbsp red wine vinegar

salt and black pepper

Method

1 Preheat the broiler to high. Toss the bread in the oil to coat evenly and spread out on a baking sheet. Grill for 1–2 minutes or until golden, turning occasionally, then leave to cool for 10 minutes.

2 Meanwhile, make the dressing. Heat the oil in a small saucepan and fry the chili, stirring, for I minute or until softened but not browned. Remove from the heat, leave to cool slightly, then add the pesto and vinegar. Whisk with a fork and season.

3 Mix the toasted bread with the tomatoes, onion, and feta. Scatter the basil over the salad. Spoon the dressing over and toss lightly to combine.

Serves 4

Fish with Tomato and Dill

Ingredients

3 medium tomatoes

1 1/2 lb/750 g freshwater fish fillets

6 cups chicken bouillon

2 tbsp chopped fresh dill

salt and pepper

extra fresh dill to garnish

Method

1 Chop the tomatoes into wedges. Cut the fish into large, bite-sized chunks. Boil the bouillon and add the fish, turn down the heat to simmer for 6 minutes. Skim the surface froth and add the tomatoes, the dill, and salt and pepper to taste.

2 Simmer a little longer until the fish is cooked but not breaking up. Serve in large bowl or individual bowls and garnish with fresh dill.

Serves 6

Iced Tomato and Pepper Soup

Ingredients

2 white onions, roughly chopped

2 large green bell peppers seeded and roughly chopped

2 cucumbers, peeled, seeded, and chopped

2 x 14 oz/400 g cans whole peeled tomatoes

3 cups canned tomato juice

lemon juice

salt and cayenne pepper

ice cubes

Method

1 Place half the onions, peppers, and cucumbers in a food processor or blender. Blend until finely chopped. Add the tomatoes and blend again. Pour the mixture into a bowl and stir in the tomato juice and lemon juice. Season with salt if required and a dash of cayenne pepper. Chill thoroughly.

2 Finely chop the remaining vegetables separately and place them in small bowls for garnish. Chill until required. Place 2 or 3 ice cubes in each soup bowl; ladle or pour the soup over. Offer the prepared garnishes separately and serve with garlic croûtons.

Serves 4

Bean Salad with Basil and Walnut Dressing

Ingredients

1 red-skinned pear, such as Forelle or blush, cored, quartered, and sliced into chunks

14 oz/400 g can flageolet beans, rinsed and drained

2¹/₂ oz/75 g prosciutto cut into strips

salt and black pepper

2 tbsp walnut pieces

Dressing

4 tbsp walnut oil

handful of fresh basil leaves

juice of 1 lime

Method

1 To make the dressing, place the walnut oil and basil in a food processor, reserving a few basil leaves for garnish, and blend until smooth. Add the lime juice and blend again to combine.

2 Mix the pear with the beans and the prosciutto. Arrange on serving plates, season to taste, and scatter with the walnuts. Drizzle the dressing over the salad and garnish with the reserved basil leaves.

Serves 4

Smoked Mackerel, Orange, and Lentil Salad

Ingredients

2 oz/55 g green lentils

4 small oranges

6 oz/170 g watercress

14 oz/400 g smoked mackerel fillet, skinned and coarsely flaked

Dressing

4 tbsp horseradish cream

4 tbsp vegetable oil

salt and black pepper

Method

1 Cook the lentils in a saucepan of boiling water for 30 minutes or until tender.

2 Meanwhile, slice the top and bottom off each orange, using a small serrated knife – work over a bowl to catch the juices. Cut away the peel and pith, following the curve of the fruit, then carefully cut between the membranes to release the segments. Squeeze the juice from the membranes into the bowl and reserve for the dressing. Arrange the watercress, orange segments, and smoked mackerel in serving bowls.

3 To make the dressing, mix together the horseradish, oil, seasoning, and the reserved orange juice. Drain the lentils, stir into the dressing, then spoon over the salad and serve.

Serves 4

Hot and Sour Scallop Soup

Ingredients

4 cups canned reduced-salt chicken bouillon

1 cup mushrooms, thinly sliced

$^1/_4$ cup bamboo shoots, sliced

$^1/_2$ lb/500 g sea or bay scallops, sliced $^1/_4$ in/5 mm thick

1 tsp reduced-salt soy sauce

$^1/_4$ tsp white pepper

2 tbsp cornstarch

3 tbsp warm, water

1 egg, beaten

3 tbsp rice vinegar (2 tbsp white wine vinegar may be substituted)

$^1/_3$ cup thinly sliced scallions

Method

1 Place the chicken bouillon, mushrooms, and bamboo shoots in a saucepan. Bring to the boil, reduce the heat and simmer for 5 minutes. Rinse the scallops under cold running water. Add scallops, soy sauce, and pepper.

2 Bring to the boil. Mix the cornstarch with the warm water. Add the cornstarch mixture and sti for a few seconds until thickened. Stir briskly with a chopstick and gradually pour in the egg. Remove from the heat. Stir in the vinegar and sprinkle with the scallions. Serve immediately.

Serves 4

Chicken Waldorf Salad

Ingredients

6 oz/170 g cooked boneless chicken breasts, skinned and diced

4 sticks celery, thinly sliced

3 oz/85 g walnuts, roughly chopped

1 red-skinned eating apple

1 green-skinned eating apple

juice of $1/2$ lemon

7 oz/200 g mixed salad leaves

snipped fresh chives to garnish

Dressing

4 tbsp reduced-fat mayonnaise

4 tbsp low-fat plain yogurt

$1/4$ tsp finely grated lemon zest

black pepper

Method

1 Place the chicken in a bowl, add the celery and walnuts, and stir to combine. Core, then dice the apples, and toss in the lemon juice to stop them browning. Add to the chicken and mix well.

2 To make the dressing, mix together the mayonnaise, yogurt, lemon rind, and black pepper in a small bowl. Spoon over the chicken mixture and toss lightly to mix. Cover and refrigerate for at least 1 hour before serving.

3 Arrange the salad leaves on serving plates and spoon the chicken mixture over. Garnish with fresh chives.

Serves 4

Waldorf Salad with Red Leicester

Ingredients

6 oz/170 g red cabbage, finely shredded

4 sticks of celery, sliced

5 oz/145 g red Leicester cheese,
  cut into 1 cm/¹/₂ in cubes

3 oz/85 g red seedless grapes, halved

2 red-skinned eating apples, cored
  and chopped

1 Romaine lettuce, leaves torn

¹/₂ tsp poppy seeds

Dressing

5 oz/145 g tub plain low-fat yogurt

2 tbsp reduced-fat mayonnaise

1 tsp fresh lemon juice or
  white wine vinegar

black pepper

Method

1 To make the dressing, mix together the yogurt, mayonnaise, lemon juice or vinegar, and seasoning. In a large bowl, combine the cabbage, celery, Red Leicester, grapes, and apples, then toss with the dressing.

2 Divide the lettuce leaves among serving plates and top with the cabbage and cheese mixture. Sprinkle with poppy seeds before serving.

Serves 4

Tomato and Mozzarella Salad

Ingredients

6 plum tomatoes, sliced

8 oz/225 g mozzarella cheese, sliced

2 scallions, sliced

3 oz/85 g black olives

salt and black pepper

Dressing

3 tbsp extra virgin olive oil

1 clove garlic, crushed

2 tsp balsamic vinegar

2 tbsp chopped fresh basil

Method

1 Arrange the tomatoes, mozzarella, scallions and olives in layers on serving plates and season.

2 To make the dressing, heat the oil and garlic in a small saucepan over a very low heat for 2 minutes or until the garlic has softened but not browned. Remove the pan from the heat, add the vinegar and basil, then pour over the salad.

Serves 4

Warm Mediterranean Pasta Shell Salad

Ingredients

6 oz/170 g dried pasta shells

5 oz/145 g fine green beans, halved

4 scallions, sliced

1 green bell pepper, deseeded
and chopped

4 oz/115 g cherry tomatoes, halved

1 large ripe avocado, halved, stoned
and peeled

black pepper

torn fresh basil leaves to garnish

Dressing

3 tbsp olive or sunflower oil

1 tbsp white wine vinegar

1 tbsp clear honey

1 tsp Dijon mustard

Method

1 To make the dressing, place the oil, vinegar, honey, and mustard in an empty screw-top jar and shake well to combine.

2 Cook the pasta shells according to the packet instructions. When they are almost cooked, add the green beans and cook for 2 minutes or until the pasta is tender but still firm to the bite and the beans have softened. Drain well.

3 Place the pasta and beans in a large bowl with the scallions, green pepper, cherry tomatoes, avocado, and seasoning. Add the dressing and toss well. Garnish with the basil.

Serves 4

Oregano Lamb and Couscous Salad

Ingredients

1 lb/455 g lamb loin

2 cloves garlic, crushed

1 tsp ground cinnamon

1 tsp ground allspice

2 tbsp lemon juice

1 tsp honey

1 tbsp olive oil

2 tbsp fresh oregano, chopped

1 cup couscous

2 cups reduced-salt chicken bouillon

**14 oz/400 g can chickpeas,
    rinsed and drained**

7 oz/200 g cherry tomatoes, halved

**2 cups fresh Italian parsley,
    roughly chopped**

1 cup raisins

2 oranges, cut into segments

Method

1 Trim the lamb loin of all excess fat and sinew. Put the garlic, cinnamon, allspice, lemon juice, honey, olive oil, and oregano in a jug and whisk to combine. Pour over the lamb, cover, and marinate in the refrigerator for 4 hours or overnight.

2 Put the couscous in a bowl. Bring the chicken bouillon to the boil and pour over the couscous. Allow to stand for 10 minutes or until all the liquid is absorbed.

3 Lightly oil a char-grill or barbecue and cook the marinated lamb loin over a medium-high heat for about 10 minutes or until medium-rare. Allow to stand for 5 minutes before slicing.

4 Fold the lamb, chickpeas, tomatoes, parsley, raisins, and oranges through the salad and serve.

Serves 4

Greek Shish Kebabs

Ingredients

1¹/₂ lb/680 g lamb neck fillet,
    cut into 1 in/2¹/₂ cm pieces
fresh mint to garnish
lemon wedges to serve

Marinade

3¹/₂ oz/100 g strained plain yogurt
¹/₂ small onion, grated
2 cloves garlic, crushed
juice of ¹/₂ lemon
1 tbsp olive oil
3 tbsp chopped fresh mint
salt and black pepper

Method

1 To make the marinade, mix together the yogurt, onion, garlic, lemon juice, oil, mint, and seasoning in a large non-metallic bowl. Add the lamb and stir to coat. Cover with plastic wrap and refrigerate for 4 hours or overnight.

2 Preheat the broiler to high. Thread the lamb onto 4 or 8 metal skewers, depending on the size of the skewers. Broil the kebabs for 10–12 minutes, turning the skewers 2–3 times, until cooked through. Garnish with mint and serve with lemon wedges.

Serves 4

Thai Beef Salad

Ingredients

1 lb/455 g round steak

black pepper

1 small red chili, finely chopped

2 tbsp lime juice

2 tbsp fish sauce

2 tbsp grated palm sugar
    or brown sugar

1 tsp sesame oil

$^1/_4$ Chinese cabbage, finely shredded

1 cup fresh cilantro sprigs

1 cup fresh mint sprigs

4 oz/115 g snow peas, trimmed

1 Lebanese cucumber, sliced

1 small red onion, thinly sliced

7 oz/200 g cherry tomatoes, halved

Method

1 Trim any excess fat and sinew from the steak. Season with black pepper.

2 Cook the steak on a lightly oiled char-grill for a few minutes until medium rare. Remove and rest for 10 minutes before slicing across the grain into thin strips.

3 Put the chili, lime juice, fish sauce, palm sugar, and sesame oil in a jug and whisk to combine.

4 Combine the cabbage, half the cilantro, the mint, snow peas, cucumber, onion, and tomatoes on a large salad platter or on individual plates.

5 Top with the sliced steak, drizzle with dressing, and garnish with the remaining cilantro.

Serves 4

Bruschetta with Bocconcini and Basil

Ingredients

1 ciabatta loaf, sliced in ³/₄ in/2 cm slices

¹/₄ cup olive oil

¹/₂ cup sun-dried tomato paste

6 oz/170 g bocconcini, each ball sliced into 5 slices

¹/₂ cup basil leaves, sliced, or whole leaves

Method

1 Grill the ciabatta slices on each side for 2–3 minutes.

2 Brush with olive oil, spread with the sun-dried tomato paste, and top with the bocconcini slices and shredded basil leaves, or whole leaves, if prefered.

Serves 6

Butterflied Quail with Lemon and Sage Leaves

Ingredients

2 tbsp olive oil

I tbsp lemon juice

$^1/_2$ tsp lemon zest

I clove garlic, crushed

freshly ground pepper

sea salt

2 tbsp olive oil, extra

4 quails, butterflied

**I bunch sage leaves, I tablespoon
   chopped; the rest for garnish**

$^1/_4$ cup chicken bouillon

Method

1 Preheat the oven to 350°F/180°C/Gas Mark 4.

2 Combine the olive oil, lemon juice, lemon zest, garlic, pepper, and salt in a bowl and set aside.

3 Heat half the extra oil in a large frying pan, add the quail and the chopped sage leaves, and brown quickly. Set aside in a baking dish.

4 To the pan, add the remaining oil, the lemon juice mixture, and the chicken bouillon. Return to the heat, bring to the boil, and simmer for I minute (to reduce the liquid), stirring with a wooden spoon.

5 Pour the pan juices over the quail and bake in the oven, for 20–25 minutes. Garnish with whole sage leaves.

Serves 4

Velvet Chicken and Corn Soup

Ingredients

1 lb/500 g boned chicken breast

large pinch of salt

2 egg whites, beaten to froth

6 cups chicken bouillon

14 oz/400 g can creamed corn

2 tbsp cornstarch blended
  with 3^1/$_2$ tbsp water

2 tbsp dry sherry

1 tsp light soy sauce

1 tsp sesame oil

thin Chinese smoked ham or
  bacon for garnish

Method

1 Remove the fat from the chicken then grind, food process, or finely chop it until it is almost a purée. Mix in the salt well and fold in the egg whites. Bring the bouillon to the boil, add the corn and return the soup to the boil. Thicken with cornstarch mix, stirring for about 1 minute.

2 Stir in the chicken purée, sherry, soy sauce, and sesame oil, and simmer, stirring, for 3 minutes. Serve the soup garnished with finely chopped ham or cooked bacon bits.

Note: If you can't buy Chinese ham, substitute Virginia ham.

Serves 6

California Rolls

Ingredients

**4 medium cooked shrimps
  or seafood sticks**

4 nori sheets

1 tbsp wasabi

1¹/₂ oz/45 g Japanese mayonnaise

4–8 coral lettuce leaves

**1 ripe avocado, peeled,
  seeded, and sliced**

1 cucumber, cut into thin slices

8 tsp flying-fish roe

Sushi Rice

¹/₄ cup rice vinegar

1¹/₂ oz/40 g superfine sugar

¹/₄ tsp salt

1 small piece of Konbu (kelp sheet)

2 cups water

Method

1 To make the sushi rice, combine the vinegar, sugar, and salt in a small saucepan and heat whilst stirring, until the sugar is dissolved (do not boil). Add the kelp and allow to soak.

2 Wash the rice and allow to drain. Place the rice and water in a large saucepan, cover, and bring to the boil. Reduce the heat and simmer, covered for 12 minutes. Remove from the heat and leave covered for 10 minutes. Transfer the rice to a large flat dish and pour the vinegar mixture over the rice, gently turning the rice to cool it.

3 To make the sushi rolls, cut 1 nori, sheet in half lengthwise. Use 2 pieces for making the sushi rolls. Place the nori, shiny side down, onto the mat. Moisten your hands with some water. Take a handful of rice from the rice-cooling tub. Evenly spread the rice over the nori.

5 With your forefinger, spread the desired amount of wasabi and mayonnaise in a strip across the rice.

6 Place shrimp strips or seafood sticks along the center of the rice, on top of the wasabi, then add a lettuce leaf, a strip of avocado, and a slice of cucumber. Lift the edge of the bamboo mat. Hold onto the mat and the filling. Wrap the mat and nori over the filling, making sure all ingredients are evenly pressed.

7 Turn the sushi over (fish-side up) and using thumb and middle finger, squeeze the rice together.

8 Remove the roll from the mat and place on a cutting board. Cut the roll in half then place the 2 halves next to each other and cut into thirds. Garnish with flying fish roe.

Makes 16 pieces

Summer Mains

Spiced Beef and Carrot Burgers

Ingredients

1 lb/500 g extra-lean ground beef

2 carrots, coarsely grated

1 cup mushrooms, finely chopped

1 large onion or 3 shallots, finely chopped

1 cup fresh whole-wheat breadcrumbs

2 tbsp tomato paste

1 medium egg, lightly beaten

1 clove garlic, crushed

2 tsp ground cumin

2 tsp ground cilantro

1 tsp hot chili powder

black pepper

Method

1 Preheat the broiler to medium. Place all the ingredients in a large bowl and mix together well.

2 Using your hands, shape the mixture into 4 round flat burgers.

3 Broil for about 10–15 minutes, until the burgers are lightly browned and cooked to your liking, turning once. Try serving them in buns piled high with crisp salad leaves, slices of tomato, and tangy relish.

Serves 4

Roasted Herb-Stuffed Chicken

Ingredients

4 chicken breasts, skin on

2 tbsp thick plain yogurt

1 clove garlic, crushed

1 tsp olive oil

2 tbsp mint, finely chopped

2 tbsp Italian parsley,
finely chopped

2 tbsp oregano, finely chopped

2 tbsp thyme, finely chopped

2 tbsp fennel, finely chopped

2 scallions, finely chopped

salt and finely ground black pepper

Method

1 In a small bowl, combine all the ingredients, except the chicken, and mix well.

2 Using your finger tips, scoop up a quarter of the mixture and gently push under the skin of the chicken. Run your fingers over the skin to smooth the stuffing out. Repeat with the remaining pieces. Cover, and refrigerate for 1 1/2 hours.

3 Pre-heat the oven to 350°F/180°C/Gas Mark 4, place the chicken on a roasting rack, and cook the chicken for 15–17 minutes. (When juices run clear, the chicken is cooked.)

Note: The herbs all need to be very finely chopped.

Serves 4–6

Spanish Seafood Paella

Ingredients

1 tbsp olive oil

2 onions, chopped

2 cloves garlic, crushed

1 tbsp fresh thyme leaves

2 tsp finely grated lemon zest

4 ripe tomatoes, chopped

2^1/$_2$ cups short-grain white rice

pinch of saffron threads,
   soaked in 2 cups water

4 cups chicken or fish bouillon

11 oz/315 g fresh or frozen peas

2 red bell peppers, chopped

2^1/$_4$ lb/1 kg mussels, scrubbed
   and beards removed

1 lb/455 g firm white fish fillets,
   chopped

11 oz/315 g peeled uncooked
   shrimps

7 oz/200 g scallops

3 squid tubes, sliced

1 tbsp chopped fresh parsley

Method

1 Preheat a hotplate or barbecue to a medium heat. Place a large paella or frying pan on the hotplate or barbecue, add the oil, and heat. Add the onions, garlic, thyme leaves, and lemon zest and cook for 3 minutes or until
the onion is soft.

2 Add the tomatoes and cook, stirring, for 4 minutes. Add the rice and cook, stirring, for 4 minutes longer or until the rice is translucent. Stir in the saffron mixture and bouillon and bring to a simmer. Simmer, stirring occasionally, for 30 minutes or until the rice has absorbed almost all of the liquid.

3 Stir in the peas, red bell pepper, and mussels, and cook for 2 minutes. Add the fish, shrimps, and scallops, and cook, stirring, for 2–3 minutes. Stir in the squid and parsley and cook, stirring, for 1–2 minutes longer or until the seafood is cooked.

Serves 8

Lamb Chops with Garlic Mayonnaise

Ingredients

6 tbsp olive oil

2 cloves garlic, minced

2 tbsp minced parsley

1 tbsp chopped fresh thyme
  or $^1/_2$ tsp dried thyme

1$^1/_2$ tbsp lemon juice

12 lamb rib chops, each $^1/_2$ in/2 cm

salt and freshly ground pepper

Quick Aioli

$^3/_4$ cup mayonnaise

1 tbsp extra-virgin olive oil

4 cloves garlic, or to taste,
  mashed through a garlic press

1 tbsp lemon juice

1 tsp mustard powder

Method

1 In a shallow bowl, mix together the oil, minced garlic, parsley, thyme, and lemon juice. Add the chops and coat well. Cover and refrigerate for at least 2 hours.

2 To make the quick aioli, whisk all the ingredients together in a small bowl.

3 Transfer to a serving bowl.

4 Drain the chops, reserving the marinade. Cook the chops under a preheated broiler or over a hot charcoal fire, basting occasionally with marinade, until browned and cooked to your taste. Season with salt and pepper. Serve with the aioli.

Serves 4

Beef with Black Bean Sauce

Ingredients

1 lb/455 g sirloin or round steak, cut into thin strips

1 clove garlic, crushed

1 small red chili, deseeded and finely chopped (optional)

1 tbsp dark soy sauce

black pepper

2 tsp cornstarch

1 tbsp white wine vinegar

2 tbsp vegetable oil

1 yellow and 1 red bell pepper, deseeded and cut into strips

1 large zucchini, cut into matchsticks

5 oz/145 g snow peas, sliced

3 tbsp black bean stir-fry sauce

4 scallions, sliced

Method

1 Combine the steak strips, garlic, chili, if using, soy sauce, and seasoning in a bowl. In another bowl, mix the cornstarch with 1 tablespoon of water until smooth, then stir in the vinegar.

2 Heat the oil in a wok or large frying pan until very hot. Add the meat and its marinade and stir-fry for 4 minutes, tossing continuously, until is seared on all sides.

3 Add the bell peppers and stir-fry for 2 minutes. Stir in the zucchini and snow peas, and cook for 3 minutes. Reduce the heat and add the cornstarch mixture and black bean sauce. Stir to mix thoroughly, then cook for 2 minutes or until the meat and vegetables are cooked through. Scatter with the scallions just before serving.

Serves 4

Japanese Beef with Horseradish Cream

Ingredients

4 round steaks, 6 oz/170 g each, trimmed of fat

4 tbsp teriyaki or soy sauce

4 tbsp olive oil

6 tbsp crème fraîche

4 tsp horseradish

2 tsp groundnut oil

7 scallions, finely sliced, plus 1 shredded scallion

2 cloves garlic, chopped

¹/₄ tsp dried crushed chilies

Method

1 Place the steaks in a non-metallic dish. Pour the teriyaki sauce and olive oil over and turn the steaks to coat. Cover and marinate for 1–2 hours in the refrigerator. Mix the crème fraîche and horseradish in a small bowl, then cover and refrigerate.

2 Heat a ridged cast-iron griddle pan over a medium to high heat. Wipe with the groundnut oil, using a folded piece of paper towel. Alternatively, heat the oil in a heavy-based frying pan. Place 2 steaks on the griddle pan, reserving the marinade, and cook for 3 minutes on each side or until cooked to your liking. Remove and keep warm. Cook the remaining 2 steaks, then remove and keep warm.

3 Place the sliced scallion, the garlic, chilies, and reserved marinade into a small saucepan and heat through. Spoon the sauce over the steaks and top with a dollop of horseradish cream and shredded scallion. Serve the rest of the horseradish cream separately.

Serves 4

Vietnamese Beef

Ingredients

1 lb/500g fillet steak

1/2 cup vegetable oil

1 cup scallions, sliced

1 lb/500g canned bamboo shoots,
   drained and sliced

pinch of salt

1 1/2 tbsp fish sauce

2 cloves garlic, minced

1/4 cup sesame seeds

Method

1 Slice the steak into thin 2 in/5 cm strips. In a frying pan, heat half the oil and stir-fry the beef for 1 minute then remove from the pan.

2 Heat the remaining oil and sauté the scallions and bamboo shoots for 3 minutes. Add the salt and fish sauce and cook, stirring, for 5 minutes. Add the garlic and cook for a further 2 minutes.

3 Return the steak to the pan and cook until just tender. Remove from the heat, add the sesame seeds, stir through, and serve

Serves 4

149

Korean Marinated Beef Strips

Ingredients

1 lb/500 g lean beef fillet,
  sliced into ¼ in/5 mm thick strips
2 scallions, chopped, plus extra
  to garnish
vegetable oil for brushing
chili sauce to serve

Marinade

2 tbsp sesame seeds
2 cloves garlic, finely chopped
1 in/2½ cm piece fresh root ginger,
  finely chopped
2 tbsp sugar
3 tbsp light soy sauce
3 tbsp dark soy sauce
1 tbsp sesame oil

Method

1 To make the marinade, heat a frying pan, then add the sesame seeds and dry-fry, stirring constantly, for 5 minutes or until golden. Grind finely, using a pestle and mortar or coffee grinder. Add the garlic, ginger, sugar, light and dark soy sauces, and oil to the sesame seeds and grind or blend to a paste, using the pestle and mortar or a food processor.

2 Mix together the beef, scallions, and marinade in a non-metallic bowl, turning to coat. Cover and marinate in the refrigerator for 4 hours.

3 Brush a ridged, cast-iron griddle pan or large, heavy-based frying pan with the oil and heat until very hot. Add the beef strips in a single layer (you may have to cook them in batches) and cook for 1–2 minutes, turning once, until browned. Serve with chili sauce, and garnished with scallions.

Serves 4

Lamb and Pepper Kebabs with Chili Sauce

Ingredients

$^1/_2$ **cup red wine**

1 tbsp olive oil

juice of $^1/_2$ lemon

1 tbsp chopped fresh rosemary

black pepper

12 oz/340 g lean boneless leg
of lamb, cut into 12 cubes

1 red and 1 yellow bell pepper, each
deseeded and cut into 8 pieces

16 button mushrooms

Sauce

14 oz/400 g can chopped tomatoes

$^1/_2$ **cup vegetable bouillon**

1 small onion, finely chopped

1 green chili, deseeded and
finely chopped

1 tbsp tomato paste

1 clove garlic, crushed

Method

1 In a non-metallic bowl, mix 4 tablespoons of the red wine, the oil, lemon juice, rosemary, and black pepper. Add the lamb, turn to coat, then cover and place in the refrigerator for 2 hours.

2 Preheat the broiler to high. Thread the lamb, peppers, and mushrooms onto 4 metal skewers, dividing evenly. Reserve the marinade.

3 Place the tomatoes, bouillon, onion, chili, tomato paste, garlic, black pepper, and the remaining wine in a saucepan and stir. Bring to the boil, then reduce the heat and simmer, uncovered, for 15–20 minutes, until the sauce has thickened, stirring occasionally. Meanwhile, broil the kebabs for 12–18 minutes, until the lamb is tender, turning occasionally and basting with the marinade. Serve with the chili sauce.

Serves 4

Char-grilled Chicken with Mango Salsa

Ingredients

4 skinless boneless chicken breasts

I tbsp olive oil

2 tbsp fish sauce

juice of $^1/_2$ lime

salt and black pepper

fresh mint to garnish, and lime wedges
to serve

Salsa

$^1/_2$ red bell pepper, deseeded
and quartered

I mango

I small red chili, deseeded and
finely chopped

I tbsp olive oil

juice of $^1/_2$ lime

I tbsp each chopped fresh
cilantro and mint

Method

I Place the chicken breasts between plastic wrap and pound with a rolling pin to flatten them slightly. Unwrap and place in a non-metallic dish. Combine the oil, fish sauce, lime juice, and seasoning and pour over the chicken. Cover and leave to marinate in the refridgerator for I hour.

2 Meanwhile, make the salsa. Preheat the broiler to high. Broil the pepper for 10 minutes, cool, then peel off the skin and dice. Peel the mango, cut the flesh away from the stone, and chop. Combine the chopped mango, pepper, chili, oil, lime juice, and herbs in a bowl and season. Cover and refrigerate.

3 Heat a ridged cast-iron griddle pan over a medium to high heat. Wipe with the marinade, using a folded piece of paper towel. Alternatively, heat I teaspoon of the marinade in a heavy-based frying pan. Add the chicken and fry for 3–5 minutes on each side, until cooked through (you may have to do this in batches). Serve with the salsa, garnished with mint and lime.

Serves 4

Tomatoes Stuffed with Pasta and Arugula

Ingredients

4 large ripe but firm
   slicing tomatoes
salt
4 oz/125 g small dried pasta shell
1 1/2 oz/45 g arugula, shredded
6 tbsp extra virgin olive oil
2 cloves garlic, sliced
1/2 tsp crushed dried chilies
4 anchovy fillets, drained
1 tbsp balsamic vinegar

Method

1 Slice off the top of each tomato, then scoop out the seeds and flesh. Sprinkle the inside with salt and leave to drain, cut-side down, on paper towels for 1 hour.

2 Cook the pasta in plenty of boiling salted water, until tender but still firm to the bite, then drain. Add the arugula and 2 tablespoons of the oil.

3 Heat the remaining oil in a frying pan and cook the garlic, chilies, and anchovies for 2 minutes or until the anchovies have disintegrated. Add to the pasta and arugula, pour in the vinegar, and mix well. Fill the tomatoes with the pasta mixture and serve at room temperature.

Serves 4

Salmon with Champ and Tomato Salad

Ingredients

2 oz/55 g fresh white breadcrumbs

6 tbsp chopped fresh basil,
  plus extra leaves to garnish

2 tbsp snipped fresh chives

4 tbsp olive oil

finely grated zest and juice of $\frac{1}{2}$ lime

4 salmon fillets, about 6 oz/170 g each

7 oz/200 g cherry tomatoes, halved

Champ

1$\frac{1}{2}$ lb/750 g potatoes, cut into
  even-sized chunks

salt and black pepper

7 fl oz/200 mL low-fat milk

1$\frac{1}{2}$ oz/45 g butter

1 bunch scallions, chopped

Method

1 First make the champ. Cook the potatoes in boiling salted water for 15 minutes or until tender. Place the milk, butter, and all but 2 tablespoons of the chopped scallions in a saucepan and heat to just below boiling point. Drain and mash the potatoes, then stir in the milk mixture and season. Keep warm.

2 Meanwhile, preheat the oven to 400°F/200°C/Gas Mark 6. Mix the breadcrumbs with half the basil and half the chives. Add 3 tablespoons of oil, the lime zest and, the seasoning. Place the salmon on a baking sheet and press the breadcrumb mixture onto the top and sides. Bake for 15 minutes or until the top is golden and the salmon is cooked.

3 While the salmon is cooking, whisk the remaining tablespoon of oil with 1 tablespoon of lime juice in a bowl, then add the tomatoes, the reserved scallions, and the remaining basil and chives. Season to taste. Serve the tomato salad with the salmon and champ, garnished with basil.

Serves 4

Noodles with Broccoli and Carrots

Ingredients

¹/₂ lb/250 g pack stir-fry noodles

3 tbsp vegetable oil

1 in/2¹/₂ cm piece fresh root ginger, finely chopped

2 red chilies, deseeded and finely chopped

4 cloves garlic, finely sliced

2 onions, thinly sliced

2 tbsp clear honey

1¹/₄ cups vegetable or chicken bouillon, or white wine

3 tbsp white wine vinegar

1¹/₄ lb/570 g broccoli, cut into florets

11 oz/310 g carrots, pared into ribbons with a vegetable peeler

snipped fresh chives to garnish

Method

1 Prepare the noodles according to the packet instructions, then drain. Heat the oil in a large wok or heavy-based frying pan, then add the ginger and chilies and stir-fry for 1–2 minutes to soften.

2 Add the garlic and onions and fry for 5–6 minutes, until the onions have browned. Stir in the honey and cook for 6–8 minutes, until the honey starts to caramelize.

3 Add the bouillon or wine and the vinegar to the onion mixture. Bring to the boil, then reduce the heat and simmer, uncovered, for 8 minutes or until the liquid has slightly reduced. Stir in the broccoli and carrots, cover, and simmer for 8–10 minutes or until the vegetables are cooked but still crunchy.

4 Stir in the noodles and mix well. Cook, stirring, for 2–3 minutes, until the noodles are hot and most of the liquid has evaporated. Sprinkle with the chives just before serving.

Serves 4

Tortilla with Corn and Sun-Dried Tomatoes

Ingredients

8 oz/225 g potatoes, thickly sliced

3 tbsp olive oil

3 tbsp canned corn, drained

**4 sun-dried tomatoes in oil, drained
  and chopped**

2 tbsp chopped fresh parsley

6 medium eggs, beaten

salt and black pepper

Method

1 Boil the potatoes for 10 minutes and leave to cool slightly. Heat the oil in a large, flameproof, heavy-based frying pan, add the potato, and fry over a high heat for 2–3 minutes, until browned and crisp. Reduce the heat, then stir in the corn and tomatoes and heat through for 1–2 minutes.

2 Preheat the broiler to medium. Add the parsley to the beaten eggs and season, then pour over the vegetables in the frying pan. Cook over a low heat for 3–4 minutes, until the omelette base is set and lightly browned.

3 Place the pan under the broiler for 1–2 minutes, until the top is set and golden. Leave to cool slightly, then cut into 4 wedges and serve with salad.

Serves 4

Bacon, Onion, and Potato Cake

Ingredients

1 ½ lb/750 g potatoes, peeled
  and coarsely grated
½ oz/15 g butter
2 tbsp vegetable oil
1 onion, chopped
6 strips rindless bacon, cut into
  ½ in/1 cm strips
1 medium egg, beaten
1 tbsp all-purpose flour
2 tbsp chopped fresh parsley
black pepper

Method

1 Place the grated potatoes in a clean kitchen towel and squeeze out any excess liquid. Heat the butter and 1 tablespoon of the oil in a non-stick frying pan. Add the onion and bacon and cook for 5–8 minutes, until the onion has softened and the bacon is cooked through. Clean the pan.

2 Place the potatoes in a large bowl. Combine the onion and bacon mixture with the egg, flour, parsley, and seasoning. Heat half the remaining oil in the frying pan, add the potato mixture, and press into a flat round with a wooden spoon. Cook over a low heat for 10 minutes or until the base is golden.

3 Carefully slide the potato cake onto a large plate. Place another large plate over the top and flip the cake so that the uncooked side is underneath. Heat the remaining oil in the pan, then carefully slide the cake back into the pan, uncooked-side down. Cook over a low heat for 10 minutes or until the base is crisp and golden.

Serves 4

Stir-Fried Noodles with Pork and Ginger

Ingredients

**2 x 9 oz/255 g packs Chinese egg
    noodles**

9 oz/255 g fresh ground pork

1 tbsp soy sauce

1 tbsp dry sherry

1 tsp cornstarch

2 tbsp vegetable oil

**2 scallions, finely chopped,
    plus extra to garnish**

**1 tsp finely grated fresh root
    ginger**

1 carrot, finely chopped

3 tablespoons black bean sauce

$^1/_2$ cup chicken bouillon

Method

1 Cook the noodles according to the packet instructions, then drain well. In a bowl, mix together the pork, soy sauce, sherry, and cornstarch. Stir well to combine.

2 Heat oil in a wok or large heavy-based frying pan, then add the scallions and ginger and stir-fry for 30 seconds. Add the pork mixture and the carrot, and stir-fry for 5–10 minutes, until the pork has browned. Stir in the black bean sauce.

3 Pour in the bouillon and bring to the boil. Add the noodles and cook, uncovered, for 3–5 minutes, until most of the liquid is absorbed and the noodles are piping hot. Garnish with the extra scallions.

Serves 4

Texan Tacos

Ingredients

8 taco shells

6–8 slices lean roast beef, diced

2 avocadoes, diced

3 tomatoes, diced

1 tbsp chopped scallion
or onion

1 clove grlic, chopped

1 tbsp lime or lemon juice

2 tbsp olive oil

6 drops Tabasco sauce

1 tsp each ground cilantro
and cumin

freshly ground pepper

1/2 cup snipped cilantro leaves

Method

1 Crisp the taco shells in a hot oven or under a preheated broiler.

2 Combine the beef, avocado, tomato, and scallion in a bowl.

3 Combine the garlic, lime or lemon juice, oil, and Tabasco, ground cilantro and cumin, and beat well. Add to the beef mixture and toss lightly to combine. Season to taste.

4 Place 3 tablespoons of beef filling in each taco shell. Top with a spoonful of mashed avocado and cilantro leaves. Serve immediately.

Serves 8

Pan-Fried Pork Steaks with Orange and Sage

Ingredients

1 tbsp olive oil

salt and black pepper

12 thin-cut pork loin steaks

1 1/4 cups chicken bouillon

finely grated zest and juice
  of 1 orange

2 tbsp dry sherry or vermouth

2 tbsp redcurrant jelly

2 tsp chopped fresh sage or
  1 tsp dried sage

Method

1 Heat the oil in a large heavy-based frying pan. Season the steaks, add 6 steaks to the pan, and fry for 4 minutes on each side or until cooked. Remove from the pan and keep warm while you fry the rest of the steaks. Add to the first batch and keep warm.

2 Add the bouillon, orange zest and juice, sherry or vermouth, and redcurrant jelly to the pan. Cook vigorously over a high heat, stirring, for 5 minutes, or until reduced by half and darkened in color.

3 Stir the sage into the sauce and season to taste. Return the steaks to the pan and heat for 1–2 minutes to warm through. Spoon the sauce over.

Serves 4

Thai Beef Stir-Fry

Ingredients

2 tbsp oil

1³/₄ lb/800 g lean steak, cut into thin, flat strips

1 piece fresh root ginger (1 in/2¹/₂ cm), sliced

2 red chilies, chopped

3 lime leaves, shredded

3 tbsp chopped cilantro

9 oz/255 g broccoli

7 oz/200 g snow peas

1 red bell pepper, cut into cubes

10 scallions, cut into 2 in/5 cm lengths

2 tsp fish sauce

³/₄ cup thick coconut milk

Method

1 Heat a wok and pour in the oil. Add the meat and stir-fry until the meat is well sealed; this should take 2–3 minutes. Add the ginger, chilies, lime leaves, and cilantro. Next, add the broccoli, snow peas, red pepper, and scallions. Continue to stir-fry for a further minute. Drizzle the fish sauce over the vegetables and stir in the coconut milk.

2 Continue to stir-fry, moving all the ingredients around the wok over a high heat for 2–3 minutes. Serve immediately with plenty of steamed jasmine rice.

Serves 4

Sesame Salmon and Noodle Stir-Fry

Ingredients

4 oz/125 g dried or fresh egg noodles

1 tbsp oil

4 cups fresh stir-fry vegetables (carrots, snow peas, broccoli, zucchini, bell peppers, mushrooms etc)

1 tsp ginger, garlic, and shallot stir-fry mix

1 tsp sesame oil

1 tbsp sesame seeds

2 tsp lime or lemon juice

1–2 tsp brown sugar

2 x 3$^1/_2$ oz/100 g cans Atlantic salmon fillet, drained

Method

1 Place the noodles in a bowl and cover with boiling water. Stand for 5 minutes. Loosen with a chopstick or the handle of a fork, then drain in a colander.

2 Heat the oil in a wok or frying pan, add the vegetables and stir-fry mix, and stir-fry for 2–3 minutes, until the vegetables are brightly colored.

3 Add the noodles and stir-fry for 2 minutes more to heat through. Add the sesame oil, sesame seeds, lime juice, and sugar and stir to combine. Spoon onto individual plates and form into nest shapes.

4 Lower the heat, add the salmon, and reheat gently. Place the salmon in the center of the noodles and serve immediately.

Serves 4

Summer Desserts

Raspberry and Elderflower Fool

Ingredients

9 oz/255 g raspberries, defrosted if frozen, plus extra to decorate

4 tbsp elderflower cordial

4 tbsp confectioner' sugar, or to taste, plus extra to dust

2¼ cups heavy cream

fresh mint to decorate

Method

1 Purée the raspberries and elderflower cordial in a food processor until smooth. Blend in the confectioners' sugar. Spoon 1 tablespoon of the mixture into each dessert glass, reserve the remaining purée and set aside.

2 Whisk the cream until it holds its shape, then gradually fold in the reserved raspberry purée.

3 Spoon the raspberry cream into the glasses and chill in the refrigerator for 30 minutes. Serve decorated with the extra raspberries and mint and dusted with confectioners' sugar.

Serves 6

Exotic Fruit Salad

Ingredients

1 large mango

3½ oz/100 g bag physalis
   (cape gooseberries)

grated zest of ½ lemon and juice of
   1 lemon

grated zest of ½ orange and juice
   of 1 orange

2 passionfruit, halved and soft pulp and
   seeds scooped out

2 tbsp clear honey or sugar

1 large ripe galia or charentais melon,
   halved, deseeded, and flesh cut into
   bite-sized cubes

9 oz/255 g black seedless grapes

2 tbsp finely chopped fresh mint
   (optional), plus extra leaves
   to decorate

Method

1 Slice off the 2 fat sides of the mango, close to the stone. Cut a criss-cross pattern across the flesh (but not the skin) of each piece with a knife. Push the skin inside out to expose the cubes of flesh and cut them off. Remove the husks from most of the physalis, reserving a few with husks on to decorate.

2 Place the lemon and orange zest and juice, the passionfruit pulp and seeds, and the honey or sugar in a bowl and mix well. Stir in the melon, grapes, and chopped mint, if using. Cover and place in the refrigerator for 2 hours to allow the flavors to develop. Just before serving, decorate with the reserved physalis and the mint leaves.

Serves 6

Raspberry Yogurt Ice

Ingredients

**12 oz/340 g raspberries, defrosted
  if frozen**

2 oz/55 g superfine sugar

11 oz/310 g low-fat raspberry yogurt

**4 oz/125 g virtually fat-free
  strained yogurt**

**fresh mint and raspberries to
  decorate**

Method

1 Place the raspberries in a food processor and blend until smooth, or use a hand blender. Press the mixture through a sieve into a bowl, discarding the pips, then add the sugar and mix well.

2 Mix in the raspberry yogurt and strained yogurt. Pour the mixture into a shallow freezer container, cover, and freeze for 2 hours. Meanwhile, put a large empty bowl into the refrigerator to chill.

3 Spoon the raspberry mixture into the chilled bowl and beat with a fork or whisk until smooth to break down the ice crystals. Return to the container, cover, and freeze for a further 4 hours or until firm.

4 Transfer to the refrigerator for 30 minutes before serving to soften. Serve scoops of raspberry ice, decorated with fresh mint and raspberries.

Serves 4

Hotcakes with Apples and Blackberries

Ingredients

12 oz/340 g cooking apples, peeled, cored, and cut into chunks

squeeze of fresh lemon juice

1¹/₂ oz/45 g superfine sugar

2 tbsp water

8 oz/225 g blackberries

1¹/₂ all-purpose flour

1¹/₂ tsp baking powder

¹/₄ tsp baking of soda

pinch of salt

2 small eggs, separated

2 tbsp vegetable oil, plus extra for frying

1 cup whole milk

5 oz/145 g crème fraîche

Method

1 Put the apples, lemon juice, ¹/₂ oz,15 g of sugar, and water into a saucepan. Bring to the boil, then simmer, covered, for 10 minutes, shaking the pan occasionally, until the apples are tender. Place in a bowl with the blackberries.

2 Sift the flour, baking powder soda, baking, and salt into a bowl, stir in the remaining sugar, and make a well in the center. Add the egg yolks, oil, and a little of the milk. Beat in gradually to make a smooth batter, then gradually beat in the rest of the milk. Whisk the egg whites until stiff (this is easiest with an electric whisk), then gradually fold into the batter.

3 Heat a large heavy-based frying pan and brush with oil. Spoon in the batter to make 3 thick pancakes (about 2–3 tablespoons each). Cook for 1–2 minutes or, until golden, then turn over and cook for a further 1–2 minutes. Keep warm while you cook 9 more pancakes. Serve them layered with the fruit and topped with a dollop of crème fraîche.

Serves 6

Mandarin and Chocolate Layers

Ingredients

3¹/₂ oz/100 g plain chocolate,
   broken into pieces

7 oz/200 mL carton crème fraîche

4 tbsp natural yogurt

finely grated zest of 1 orange

5 oz/145 g low-fat digestive cookies

2 x 11 oz/310 g cans mandarin
   segments, drained

Method

1 Melt the chocolate in a bowl placed over a saucepan of simmering water, then leave to cool for 5 minutes. Add the crème fraîche, yogurt, and orange zest, reserving a few strips for decoration, and mix well.

2 Put the cookies into a plastic bag and roughly crush with a rolling pin. Divide half the crushed cookies among 4 dessert glasses, then top with a layer of the chocolate mixture.

3 Spoon in the mandarins, reserving a few for decoration, then sprinkle the remaining crushed cookies over the top. Top with the remaining chocolate mixture and the reserved mandarins and decorate with the reserved orange zest.

Serves 6

Gooseberries with Elderflower Syllabub

Ingredients

4 oz/125 g super fine sugar

2–3 strips lemon zest, pared with a vegetable peeler

$^1/_2$ cup water

11 oz/310 g gooseberries, topped and tailed

Syllabub

finely grated zest and juice of 1 lemon

3 tbsp sweet muscat wine

$^1/_2$ tsp freshly grated nutmeg

$^1/_4$ tsp ground ginger

1 cup heavy cream

4 tbsp elderflower cordial

superfine sugar, to taste

Method

1 Place the lemon zest, and juice, and the muscat, nutmeg and ginger for the syllabub in a bowl. Cover and place in the refrigerator for 8 hours, or overnight.

2 Place the sugar, lemon strips, and water in a heavy-based saucepan and bring to the boil, stirring to dissolve the sugar. Add the gooseberries and bring back to the boil. Reduce the heat and simmer for 5–8 minutes, until the gooseberries are tender. Transfer the gooseberries to a bowl. Boil the syrup for 3 minutes or until thick and sticky. Leave to cool for 1–2 minutes, then strain over the gooseberries. Leave to cool for 20 minutes.

3 Strain the syllabub mixture into a large bowl, add the cream, and whisk. Gradually whisk in the cordial, then continue whisking until the mixture is thick but not too stiff. Add the superfine sugar to taste. Spoon the gooseberry mixture into glasses, then top with the syllabub.

Serves 4

The days are becoming shorter, leaves rustle underfoot, and a there is a slight chill in the air. In the fall you'll find some wonderfully versatile seasonal ingredients which include apples, cabbage, grapes, greens, pears, persimmons, pomegranates, beets, pumpkins, spinach, sweet potatoes, and turnips. In our fall section there are recipes for heart-warming appetizers, such as Broiled Sardines with Orange and Dill Relish; toasty snacks and a hot soufflé; tasty meat dishes with rich sauces, such as Beef Fillet with Wild Mushrooms; and hot fruit desserts, including Red Berry and Banana Pie.

Fall

Fall Appetizers, Snacks, & Salads

Gnocchi with Mascarpone and Blue Cheese

Ingredients

14 oz/400 g fresh gnocchi

1 tbsp pine nut kernels

4 oz/115 g mascarpone

4 oz/115 g pack blue cheese, crumbled

salt and black pepper

Method

1 Cook the gnocchi according to the packet instructions. Drain well, then transfer to a shallow flameproof dish.

2 Preheat the broiler to high. Place the pine nut kernels under the broiler and toast for 2–3 minutes, stirring from time to time, until golden. (Keep an eye on them as they can burn quickly.)

3 Meanwhile, put the mascarpone and blue cheese in a saucepan and warm over a very low heat, stirring, until melted. Season to taste. Spoon over the gnocchi, then broil for 2–3 minutes until bubbling and golden. Scatter the pine nut kernels over the top and serve.

Serves 4

Broiled Sardines with Orange and Dill Relish

Ingredients

12 fresh sardines, scaled and gutted

3 tbsp olive oil

finely grated zest of 1 orange

salt and black pepper

Relish

4 large oranges

bunch of scallions, finely sliced

1–2 red chilies, deseeded and
finely chopped

3 tbsp chopped dill, plus
extra to garnish

2 tbsp capers, rinsed
and drained

1–2 tbsp extra virgin olive oil

Method

1 Slash the sardines diagonally, 3 or 4 times on each side, using a sharp knife. Mix together the oil, orange zest, and seasoning, add the sardines, and turn to coat. Cover and place in the refrigerator for 30 minutes.

2 Meanwhile, make the relish. Slice the top and bottom off each orange with a sharp knife, then cut off the skin and pith, following the curve of the fruit. Cut between the membranes to release the segments, then chop into $^1/_2$ in/1 cm pieces. Mix with the scallions, chilies, dill, capers, and oil.

3 Preheat the broiler to high. Put the sardines onto the broiler rack, reserving the marinade. Broil, brushing occasionally with the marinade, for 3 minutes on each side or until the flesh has turned opaque and the skin has browned. Garnish with dill and serve with the relish.

Serves 6

Indian Spiced Potato and Onion Soup

Ingredients

1 tbsp vegetable oil

1 onion, finely chopped

$^{1}/_{2}$ in/1 cm piece fresh root ginger,
  finely chopped

2 large potatoes, cut into
  $^{1}/_{2}$ in/1 cm in cubes

2 tsp ground cumin

2 tsp ground cilantro

$^{1}/_{2}$ tsp turmeric

1 tsp ground cinnamon

4 cups chicken bouillon

salt and black pepper

1 tbsp plain yogurt to garnish

Method

1 Heat the oil in a large saucepan. Fry the onion and ginger for 5 minutes or until softened. Add the potatoes and fry for another minute, stirring often.

2 Mix the cumin, cilantro, turmeric, and cinnamon with 2 tablespoons of cold water to make a paste. Add to the onion and potato, stirring well, and fry for 1 minute to release the flavors.

3 Add the bouillon and season to taste. Bring to the boil, then reduce the heat, cover, and simmer for 30 minutes or until the potato is tender. Blend until smooth in a food processor or press through a metal sieve. Return to the pan and gently heat through. Garnish with the yogurt and more black pepper.

Serves 4

Broccoli Soufflés with Olive Purée

Ingredients

butter for greasing
1 lb/455 g broccoli, chopped
10 fl oz/ 285 mL carton light cream
4 medium eggs, separated
salt and black pepper

Olive Purée
20 pitted black olives
4 fl oz/115 mL olive oil
grated zest and juice of 1 lemon

Method

1 Preheat the oven to 425°F/220°C/Gas Mark 7. Grease 4 individual ramekin dishes. Cook the broccoli in a little boiling salted water for 15 minutes or until tender, then drain well. Using a food processor, to a smooth purée with the cream, egg yolks, and seasoning. Transfer to a large mixing bowl.

2 Beat the egg whites until they increase in volume six-fold and form soft peaks. Gently fold one-third of the beaten whites into the broccoli purée using a large metal spoon. Carefully fold in the remaining whites in 2 batches, mixing well.

3 Divide the mixture among the ramekin dishes and cook for 20–25 minutes, until risen and golden. Meanwhile, purée the olives, olive oil, and lemon zest and juice in a food processor or with a hand blender. Serve with the hot soufflés.

Serves 4

Sun-Dried Tomato and Cheese Puffs

Ingredients

3 oz/80 g butter

1 cup water

6 oz/170 g all-purpose flour, sifted

1/2 tsp salt

4 medium eggs, beaten

6 oz/170 g Gruyère cheese, grated

Stuffing

2 oz/55 g sun-dried tomatoes in oil, drained

2 oz/55 g butter

Method

1 Preheat the oven to 400°F/200°C/Gas Mark 6. Gently heat the butter and of water in a large saucepan for 5 minutes or until the butter has melted. Bring to the boil, then remove from the heat and stir in the flour and salt. Beat with a wooden spoon until the mixture forms a smooth ball.

2 Gradually add the eggs, beating well, until the dough is shiny. Stir in the Gruyère. Place balls of the dough (about 2 tablespoons each) onto a baking sheet and cook for 20 minutes or until risen and browned. Turn off the oven. Cut a slit in the top of each puff to let the steam escape. Return the puffs to the cooling oven for 5 minutes, then remove and cool for a further 5 minutes.

3 Meanwhile, make the stuffing. Place the tomatoes and butter in a food processor and blend to a paste. Divide the paste among the puffs, packing it in with a teaspoon.

Serves 4

Spicy Cheese and Onion Rarebit

Ingredients

1 oz/30 g butter

1 small red onion, finely chopped

8 oz/225 g mature Cheddar, grated

¹/₂ tsp cayenne pepper

dash of Worcestershire sauce

3 tbsp cider, beer, or milk

4 thick slices white bread

Method

1 Preheat the broiler to high. Melt the butter in a saucepan over a low heat, then fry the onion for 5 minutes or until softened. Add the Cheddar, cayenne pepper, Worcestershire sauce, and cider, beer, or milk, then bring to a simmer, stirring. When the Cheddar has just melted, remove from the heat.

2 Meanwhile, toast the bread on both sides. Divide the Cheddar mixture among the slices of toast, then broil for 3 minutes or until the topping starts to turn brown.

Serves 4

Mixed Vegetable and Bean Soup

Ingredients

2 tbsp olive oil

1 onion, finely chopped

2 cloves garlic, crushed

1 potato, finely diced

1 carrot, finely diced

2 tsp cumin seeds

4 cups vegetable bouillon

2 sticks celery, finely chopped

1 large zucchini, finely chopped

4 oz/125 g fine green beans,
  cut into 1 in/2¹/₂ cm pieces

15 oz/425 g can wax beans, drained

14 oz/400 g can chopped tomatoes

black pepper

2 oz/55 g Cheddar cheese, grated

Method

1 Heat the oil in a large heavy-based saucepan, then add the onion, garlic, potato, carrot, and cumin seeds. Cook, uncovered, for 5 minutes, stirring from time to time, until the vegetables have softened.

2 Add the bouillon, celery and zucchini and bring to the boil. Cover and simmer for 10 minutes or until the celery and zucchini are tender.

3 Stir in the green beans, wax beans, chopped tomatoes, and plenty of seasoning. Simmer, uncovered, for 5 minutes or until the green beans are tender. Pour the soup into bowls and top with the grated Cheddar.

Serves 4

Caramelized Shallots and Asparagus Toasts

Ingredients

3 tbsp olive oil

10¹/₂ oz/300 g shallots, thickly sliced

2 cloves garlic, thickly sliced

1 red chili, deseeded and
   sliced (optional)

1¹/₂ tbsp soft dark brown sugar

2 tbsp dark soy sauce

1 tbsp white wine vinegar
   or cider vinegar

¹/₂ cup white wine

3¹/₂ oz/100 g asparagus tips

4 plum tomatoes

juice of ¹/₂ lemon

12 thick slices French bread

Italian parsley or cilantro
   to garnish

Method

1 Heat the oil in a wok or large, heavy-based frying pan. Add the shallots, garlic, and chili, if using, and stir-fry for 4–5 minutes, until they start to color. Add the sugar and the soy sauce and stir-fry for 3–4 minutes, until the shallots are evenly browned.

2 Add the vinegar and wine to the shallots and bring to the boil. Reduce the heat and simmer, uncovered, for 8 minutes or until the shallots have softened and the liquid has thickened and looks glossy. Add the asparagus, cover, and cook for 4–5 minutes, until tender, stirring occasionally.

3 Place the tomatoes in a bowl and cover with boiling water. Leave for 30 seconds, then peel, deseed, and chop. Add to the asparagus, along with the lemon juice, then stir and heat for 1–2 minutes.

4 Meanwhile, preheat the broiler to high. Toast the bread on both sides. Serve the toasts topped with the vegetable mixture and garnished with the parsley or cilantro.

Serves 6

Manhattan Oyster Chowder

Ingredients

2 tbsp olive oil

1 onion, chopped into bite-sized chunks

4$^1/_2$ oz/125 g dark-gilled mushrooms, quartered

2 cloves garlic, chopped

3 cups fish bouillon

16 oz/455 g can tomatoes, seeded and chopped

bay leaf

$^1/_4$ tsp rosemary, crushed to a powder

$^1/_4$ tsp oregano, crushed to a powder

pinch of hot pepper flakes

1 zucchini, cut into bite-sized chunks

1 jar standard oysters

parsley

Method

1 Heat the oil in large saucepan and sauté the onions and mushrooms until the onions are golden and the mushrooms are brown. Add the garlic and stir for 1 minute. Add the fish bouillon, chopped tomatoes, and the juice reserved from the can of tomatoes. Stir in the bay leaf, rosemary, oregano, and hot pepper flakes. Bring to a boil, then reduce the heat and simmer, partially covered, for 25 minutes.

2 Add the zucchini, cover, and simmer for another 10 minutes or until the zucchini is almost tender. Slip the oysters with their liquid into the soup and cook, uncovered, just until the edges of the oysters begin to curl. (You want them tender, not chewy.)

3 Ladle the soup into bowls. Sprinkle with parsley and serve immediately.

Note: Fat, dense oyster biscuits taste very good with this soup.

Serves 4

Chef's Autumn Salad

Ingredients

salt and black pepper

8 oz/225 g broccoli, cut into
   small florets

1 Romaine lettuce, leaves torn

1 red onion, halved and sliced

1/2 cucumber, peeled and diced

2 sticks celery, sliced

2 carrots, cut into matchsticks

2 apples, diced

7 oz/200 g wafer-thin cooked turkey
   or ham slices

2 tbsp each raisins and roasted
   salted peanuts, chopped (optional)

Dressing

1 tsp Dijon mustard

juice of 1/2 lime

5 oz/145 g carton low-fat plain yogurt

2 tbsp olive oil

1 tbsp chooped fresh cilantro

salt and black pepper

Method

1 Bring a large saucepan of salted water to the boil. Add the broccoli, return to the boil, then cook for 1–2 minutes or until slightly softened. Drain and leave to cool for 15 minutes. Meanwhile, make the dressing. Mix together the mustard, lime juice, yogurt, oil, cilantro, and seasoning.

2 Place the lettuce, red onion, cucumber, broccoli, celery, carrots, and apples in a large bowl. Pour the dressing over and toss to coat. Arrange the turkey or ham slices in the center of a shallow serving dish or platter and spoon the salad around the edge. Scatter with the raisins and peanuts, if using.

Serves 6

Coconut, Sweet Potato, and Spinach Soup

Ingredients

I oz/30 g butter

I lb/455 g sweet potatoes,
   cut into ¹/₂ in/I cm dice

I onion, chopped

2 cloves garlic, crushed

I tsp grated fresh root ginger

I tbsp medium curry paste

2¹/₂ cups vegetable bouillon

I cup coconut milk

juice of I lime

¹/₄ tsp dried crushed chilies

6 oz/I70 g fresh spinach, shredded

salt and black pepper

Method

1 Melt the butter in a saucepan and fry the potatoes, onion, garlic, ginger, and curry paste for 5 minutes or until lightly golden.

2 Add the bouillon, coconut milk, lime juice, and chili. Bring to the boil, cover, and simmer for 15 minutes or until the potatoes are tender.

3 Leave the soup to cool a little, then purée half of it with a hand blender. Return the purée to the pan, add the spinach, and cook for 1–2 minutes, until the spinach has just wilted and the soup has heated through. Season to taste.

Serves 4

Spinach and Nutmeg Soup with Cheese Toasts

Ingredients

2 tbsp olive oil

1 oz/30 g butter

9 oz/255 g floury potatoes, such as King Edward, peeled and cut into 1 in/2½ cm cubes

9 oz/255 g spinach leaves

1 tsp freshly grated nutmeg

6 cups chicken or vegetable bouillon

salt and black pepper

4 tbsp crème fraîche

3½ oz/100 g Gruyère, Caerphilly or Cheddar cheese, grated

1 large egg, beaten

day-old narrow French bread stick, cut diagonally into 18 x ½ in/1 cm slices

Method

1 Heat the oil and half the butter in a large saucepan. Fry the potatoes for 1 minute, then add the spinach and nutmeg. Cook for 2 minutes or until the spinach is wilting.

2 Add the bouillon, season lightly, and bring to the boil. Reduce the heat, cover, and simmer for 10–15 minutes or until the potatoes are tender. Leave to cool for 10 minutes.

3 Pour the soup into a food processor and blend until smooth, or use a hand blender. Stir in half the crème fraîche, then adjust the seasoning to taste. Set aside.

4 Preheat the broiler. Mix the grated cheese with the egg and the rest of the crème fraîche. Lightly toast the bread slices, then spread the cheese mixture over one side of each slice. Dot with the rest of the butter and season with a little black pepper. Broil for 5 minutes or until bubbling and golden. Heat the soup through and serve topped with the cheese toasts.

Serves 6

Thick Minestrone with Pesto

Ingredients

3 tbsp olive oil

1 onion, chopped

2 cloves garlic, chopped

1 potato, cut into ¹/₂ in/1 cm cubes

2 small carrots, cut into ¹/₂ in/1 cm in cubes

1 large zucchini, cut into ¹/₂ in/1 cm cubes

¹/₄ white cabbage, chopped

3 cups vegetable bouillon

2 x 14 oz/400 g cans chopped tomatoes

3 oz/85 g pasta shapes, such as shells (conchiglie)

salt and black pepper

4 tbsp grated Parmesan cheese

4 tbsp pesto

Method

1 Place the oil in a large heavy-based saucepan, then add the onion, garlic, potato, carrots, zucchini, and cabbage and cook for 5–7 minutes, until slightly softened.

2 Add the bouillon and tomatoes and bring to the boil. Reduce the heat and simmer for 20 minutes, then add the pasta shapes and seasoning and cook for a further 15 minutes or until the pasta is tender but still firm to the bite. Divide the soup among serving bowls and top each serving with a tablespoon of Parmesan and pesto.

Serves 4

Fall Mains

Braised Pork with Apples

Ingredients

1 tbsp sunflower oil

4 boneless lean pork loin steaks or loin
  medallions, about 3$\frac{1}{2}$ oz/100 g each

4 shallots, thinly sliced

6 oz/170 g mushrooms, sliced

1 tbsp all-purpose flour

7 fl oz/200 mL vegetable bouillon

$\frac{1}{2}$ cup dry apple cider

2 tsp Dijon or wholegrain mustard

black pepper

2 large eating apples, peeled,
  cored, and sliced

fresh Italian parsley to garnish

Method

1 Preheat the oven to 350°F/180°C/Gas Mark 4. Heat the oil in a non-stick frying pan. Add the pork and cook for 5 minutes or until browned, turning once, then transfer to a casserole dish.

2 Add the shallots and mushrooms to the frying pan and cook gently for 5 minutes or until softened. Add the flour and cook for 1 minute, stirring. Slowly add the bouillon and cider, stirring until smooth, then add the mustard and black pepper. Bring to the boil and continue stirring for 2–3 minutes or until thickened.

3 Place the apple slices on top of the pork steaks and pour the sauce over. Cover and cook in the oven for 1–1$\frac{1}{4}$ hours until the pork is tender and cooked through. Garnish with fresh parsley.

Serves 4

Marmalade-Glazed Stuffed Turkey Steaks

Ingredients

3 turkey steaks, about 9 oz/255 g each

6 strips streaky bacon

oil for greasing

3 tbsp marmalade

1–2 tbsp whiskey (optional)

Stuffing

9 oz/255 g sausage meat

grated zest of $^1/_2$ orange

1 stick celery, finely chopped

**2 oz/55 g cranberries, defrosted if frozen
  and roughly chopped**

**4 tbsp medium matzo meal
  or fresh breadcrumbs**

1–2 tbsp chopped fresh tarragon

salt and black pepper

Method

1 Preheat the oven to 375°F/190°C/Gas Mark 5. To make the stuffing, place the sausage meat in a bowl with the orange zest, celery, cranberries, matzo meal or breadcrumbs, tarragon, and seasoning. Mix together well.

2 Place the turkey steaks between 2 sheets of plastic wrap and flatten with a rolling pin to a thickness of $^1/_4$ in/5 mm. Cut each steak in half. Divide the stuffing into 6 sausage-shaped portions; place a portion on each piece of turkey and roll up. Stretch a bacon strip around each roll, secure with a wetted cocktail stick, and place in a greased ovenproof dish.

3 Put the marmalade into a small saucepan and heat for 5 minutes or until melted. Remove from the heat and stir in the whiskey, if using. Brush half the mixture over the turkey rolls. Cook, uncovered, for 20 minutes, basting with the pan juices halfway through cooking.

4 Increase the heat to 450°F/230°C/Gas Mark 8. Brush the steaks with the remaining marmalade mixture and cook for 5 minutes or until browned and cooked through. Slice into $^1/_2$ in/1 cm medallions and drizzle over any pan juices to serve.

Serves 6

Chicken and Broccoli Lasagne

Ingredients

3 1/2 cups low-fat milk

2 shallots, sliced

2 sticks celery, sliced

2 bay leaves

8 oz/225 g broccoli, cut into
   small florets

2 tbsp sunflower oil

1 onion, chopped

1 clove garlic, crushed

8 oz/225 g mushrooms, sliced

2 zucchinis, sliced

1 1/2 oz/45 g margarine or butter

1 1/2 oz/45 g all-purpose flour

4 oz/115 g reduced-fat mature
   Cheddar, finely grated

11 oz/310 g cooked boneless chicken
   breasts, skinned and diced

black pepper

6 oz/170 g green-egg lasagne
   green sheets

Method

1 Put the milk, shallots, celery, and bay leaves into a small saucepan and bring to the boil. Set aside to infuse for 20 minutes. Cook the broccoli florets in a saucepan of boiling water for 2 minutes. Drain and set aside. Heat the oil in a frying pan and cook the onion, garlic, mushrooms, and zucchinis for 5 minutes or until softened. Set aside.

2 Preheat the oven to 350°F/180°C/Gas Mark 4. Put the margarine or butter and flour in a saucepan and strain in the milk, then bring to the boil, whisking. Simmer for 3 minutes, stirring until thickened. Set aside 1/2 pint/300 mL of the sauce and stir 3 1/2 oz/100 g of the Cheddar, the onion mixture, broccoli, chicken, and black pepper into the remaining sauce.

3 Spoon half the chicken mixture into a shallow ovenproof dish. Cover with half the lasagne sheets. Repeat, then pour the reserved sauce over and sprinkle with the rest of the Cheddar. Cook for 45 minutes or until golden.

Serves 4

Beef Fillet with Wild Mushrooms

Ingredients

¹/₂ oz/15 g dried porcini mushrooms

3 oz/85 g butter

4 beef fillet steaks, about 6 oz/170 g each

9 oz/255 g mixed fresh wild mushrooms, sliced

1 clove garlic, crushed

1 tsp chopped fresh thyme, plus extra to garnish

3 fl oz/85mL red wine

3 fl oz/85 mL beef bouillon

salt and black pepper

Method

1 Preheat the oven to 160°C/325°F/Gas Mark 3. Cover the dried mushrooms with 3 fl oz/85 mL of boiling water. Soak for 15 minutes or until softened. Strain, reserving the soaking liquid, then chop the mushrooms. Melt 1 oz/30 g of the butter in a heavy-based frying pan and fry the steaks for 2–3 minutes on each side, until browned. Wrap loosely in foil and keep warm in the oven.

2 Add 1 oz/30 g of the butter to the pan and fry the fresh mushrooms, dried mushrooms, garlic, and thyme for 4 minutes or until the fresh mushrooms have softened. Add the wine, increase the heat, and boil for 1–2 minutes, until the sauce has reduced by half.

3 Mix the dried mushroom soaking liquid with the beef bouillon, then add to the pan and simmer for 3 minutes. Stir in the remaining butter and season. Serve with the steaks, garnished with thyme.

Serves 4

Monk Fish and Proscuitto

Ingredients

3 tbsp extra virgin olive oil

4 large bell peppers (red, green, orange, or yellow), deseeded and thickly sliced

4 cloves garlic, chopped

2 sprigs fresh thyme

salt and black pepper

4 monk fish fillets, about 7 oz/200 g each

4 slices prosciutto

2 tbsp balsamic vinegar

chopped fresh basil to garnish

Method

1 Heat 2 tablespoons of the oil in a large heavy-based saucepan, then add the peppers, garlic, thyme, 2 tablespoons of water, and the seasoning. Cook, partially covered, for 20 minutes or until softened and browned, stirring occasionally.

2 Meanwhile, season the monk fish well, then wrap a slice of prosciutto around each fillet. Secure the prosciutto with a wetted cocktail stick. Heat the remaining oil in a large heavy-based frying pan, add the fillets, and fry for 8–10 minutes, turning once, until browned and cooked through. Cover loosely with foil and set aside.

3 Add the balsamic vinegar to the peppers in the pan and cook for 5 minutes to warm through. Remove the cocktail sticks, then cut the monk fish into thick slices and garnish with the fresh basil. Serve with the peppers and any pan juices.

Serves 4

Monk Fish in Cream, Wine, and Leek Sauce

Ingredients

1 stalk lemon grass

2 tbsp olive oil

salt and black pepper

2³/₄ lb/1¹/₄ kg monk fish fillet, cut into 2 in/5 cm chunks

2 leeks, white parts only, sliced into thin rings

1 scallion, chopped

large pinch of saffron threads

1 cup dry white wine

3 fl oz/85 mL heavy cream

4 tsp lemon juice

2 tbsp chopped fresh parsley

Method

1 Peel the covering from the lemon grass and finely chop the lower white bulbous part, discarding the fibrous top.

2 Heat the oil in a large, heavy-based saucepan. Season the fish with pepper, add to the oil, and cook on one side for 3 minutes or until it is starting to turn opaque. Turn the fish over, add the leeks, scallion, saffron, wine, and lemon grass. Bring the liquid to a simmer, then cover and cook for 8 minutes or until the fish is cooked through.

3 Transfer the fish and leeks to a serving dish and keep warm. Bring the sauce to the boil, then reduce the heat, add the cream, and simmer for 8–10 minutes, until reduced by a third. Remove from the heat, add the lemon juice, and season. Pour over the fish and sprinkle with parsley.

Serves 6

Moroccan Potato Casserole

Ingredients

3 tbsp olive oil

2 onions, sliced

3 cloves garlic, chopped

2 red chilies, finely chopped

1 tsp ground cumin

1 tsp ground cilantro

2 lb/900 g waxy potatoes,
such as Charlotte, cut into
¼ in/5 mm thick slices

grated zest of 1 lemon, and juice of
1 or 2 lemons

3⅔ cups vegetable bouillon

salt and black pepper

4 tbsp sour cream to serve
and 3 tbsp chopped fresh
parsley to garnish

Method

1 Preheat the oven to 400°F/200°C/Gas Mark 6. Heat the oil in a flameproof and ovenproof casserole dish. Add the onions, garlic, chilies, cumin, and cilantro, then gently fry for 1–2 minutes to release their flavors.

2 Stir in the potatoes, lemon zest, and lemon juice to taste, then add the bouillon and seasoning. Bring to the boil, cover, then cook in the oven for 40 minutes or until the vegetables are tender and the liquid has reduced slightly.

3 Transfer to plates and top each serving with a spoonful of sour cream. Sprinkle with fresh parsley to garnish.

Serves 4

Mushroom and Black Olive Risotto

Ingredients

1 oz /30 g dried porcini mushrooms

3 tbsp olive oil

1 onion, chopped

8 oz/225 g large open mushrooms, chopped

9 oz/255 g risotto rice

2 cups vegetable bouillon

2 tbsp black olives, pitted and roughly chopped

salt and black pepper

2 tbsp black olive paste

fresh Parmesan cheese to serve

Method

1 Cover the porcini with 1 cup boiling water, then leave to soak for 20 minutes. Drain, reserving the water, and set aside. Heat the oil in a large heavy-based saucepan, add the onion and fresh mushrooms, and fry for 4–5 minutes. Add the rice and stir to coat with the oil. Fry for 1–2 minutes.

2 Add the porcini and the reserved liquid to the rice with 1 cup of the vegetable bouillon and the olives. Simmer, covered, for 10 minutes or until the liquid has been absorbed, stirring occasionally.

3 Stir in $\frac{1}{2}$ cup of the remaining bouillon and cook for 5 minutes, covered, until absorbed. Add the rest of the bouillon, the seasoning, and the olive paste and cook for 5 minutes, uncovered, stirring constantly. Remove from the heat and leave to rest, covered, for 5 minutes. Shave the Parmesan over the top, using a vegetable peeler, then serve.

Serves 4

Rich Bean Stew

Ingredients

4 oz/115 g dried porcini mushrooms

3 tbsp olive oil

8 oz/225 g large open mushrooms, chopped

2 carrots, finely diced

1 large potato, diced

8 oz/225 g fine green beans, chopped

$^1\!/_2$ tbsp dried thyme

$^1\!/_2$ tbsp dried sage

2 cloves garlic, crushed

1 cup red wine

$2^1\!/_2$ cups vegetable bouillon

salt and black pepper

8 oz/225 g frozen fava beans

10 oz/285 g can cannellini beans

8 oz/225 g can flageolet beans

Method

1 Cover the porcini with $2^1\!/_4$ cups of boiling water, then soak for 20 minutes. Meanwhile, heat the oil in a large saucepan, then add the fresh mushrooms, carrots, potato, and green beans and fry gently for 3–4 minutes, until slightly softened.

2 Add the thyme, sage, and garlic, the porcini with their soaking liquid, and the red wine, bouillon and seasoning. Bring to the boil, then simmer, uncovered, for 20 minutes or until the vegetables are tender.

3 Stir in the fava beans and simmer for a further 10 minutes or until tender. Drain and rinse the cannellini and flageolet beans, add to the mixture, then simmer for 2–3 minutes to heat through.

Serves 4

Fall Desserts

Fruity Plum Toasties

Ingredients

4 thick of slices fruit bread, brioche, cinnamon bread, or chollah

1–2 tbsp plum jelly

¼ tsp ground cinnamon

1 oz/30 g superfine sugar

8–12 ripe red plums, halved and stoned

Method

1   Preheat the broiler to high. Toast the bread slices very lightly on both sides. Spread one side of the toast with the jelly, then place the slices in a single layer in a flameproof dish, jelly-side up.

2   Mix together the cinnamon and sugar. Arrange the plums on top of the toast and sprinkle with the cinnamon sugar. Place under the broiler and cook for 2–3 minutes, until the sugar begins to melt and the plums are warmed through. Leave to cool slightly before serving.

Serves 4

Red Fruit and Custard Filo Parcels

Ingredients

8 large sheets fresh filo pastry, cut in half

1 oz/30 g butter, melted, plus extra for greasing

2 oz/55 g each of fresh raspberries and blackberries

$1/2$ tbsp soft light-brown sugar

4 tbsp ready-made custard

fresh raspberries or blackberries to decorate and confectioners' sugar to dust

Fruit Sauce

2 oz/55 g each of fresh raspberries and blackberries

1 tbsp superfine sugar

Method

1 Preheat the oven to 425°F/220°C/Gas Mark 7. Lightly grease a baking sheet. Brush 3 half-sheets of pastry with the melted butter. Stack them on top of each other, buttered-sides up, then place an unbuttered half on top. Repeat with the remaining pastry sheets to make 4 wrappings for the parcels.

2 Mix the raspberries and blackberries with the brown sugar. Spoon 1 tablespoon of custard on top of each pastry stack and brush the edges with butter. Top the custard with a little fruit mixture and gather in the pastry sides, squeezing together to seal. Place on the baking sheet, brush with the remaining butter, and cook for 7–10 minutes until golden.

3 To make the fruit sauce, press the fruit through a sieve and stir in the sugar to taste. Place the parcels on plates and spoon the sauce around the pastry. Decorate with the fresh raspberries or blackberries and dust with confectioners' sugar.

Serves 4

Cranachan with Raspberries

Ingredients

1 oz/30 g butter

1¹/₂ oz/45 g soft dark brown sugar

4 oz/115 g porridge oats

7 oz/200 g ricotta

¹/₂ cup heavy cream

1–2 tbsp clear honey, plus extra for trickling (optional)

1–2 tbsp whiskey

8 oz/225 g raspberries

2 tbsp confectioners' sugar

Method

1 Preheat the oven to 325°F/160°C/Gas Mark 3. Melt the butter and sugar in a small saucepan over a low heat, then stir in the oats until well mixed. Turn onto a baking sheet and spread out. Bake for 15 minutes, stirring halfway through, until lightly toasted. Transfer to a plate and leave to cool while you prepare the cream mixture.

2 Beat the ricotta until smooth. Whisk the cream until it forms soft peaks, then fold into the ricotta with 1–2 tablespoons of honey and the whiskey to taste. Toss the fruit in the confectioners' sugar.

3 Spoon the ricotta mixture into bowls, top with the oats, and finish with the raspberries. Trickle the extra honey over, if using.

Serves 4

Caramelized Rice Pudding with Apricots

Ingredients

3 oz/85 g pudding rice

7 oz/200 g superfine sugar

**2 vanilla pods, I split in
half lengthways**

I oz/30 g sweet butter

2¹/₄ cups whole milk

5 fl oz/145 mL carton heavy cream

**2 strips lemon zest and juice
of I lemon**

7 fl oz/200 mL water

**9 oz/250 g ready-to-eat
dried apricots**

**I–2 tbsp orange liqueur,
such as Cointreau**

Method

I Put the rice into a saucepan, cover with water, and boil for 5 minutes. Drain. Return the rice to the pan with 45 g/1¹/₂ oz of the sugar, the split vanilla pod, butter, and milk. Simmer for 45–60 minutes, stirring often, until thickened. Transfer to a bowl and cool for 20 minutes. Remove the vanilla pod, and scrape the seeds into the rice. Discard the pod. Whisk the cream until it forms soft peaks, then fold into the rice.

2 Meanwhile, put 3¹/₂ oz/100 g of the sugar into a saucepan with the lemon strips, remaining vanilla pod, and the water. Heat, stirring, for 3 minutes or until the sugar dissolves. Add the apricots and cook for 20 minutes to reduce the syrup.

3 Put the apricots into 4 ramekins, add the lemon juice, liqueur and syrup, then cool for 5 minutes. Top with the rice pudding, then refrigerate for I hour. Preheat the broiler to high. Sprinkle the puddings with the rest of the sugar. Broil for 1–2 minutes or until the sugar caramelizes, then cool for a few minutes.

Serves 4

Little Pots of Chocolate

Ingredients

**2 x 3$^{1}/_{2}$ oz/100 g bars luxury bittersweet
  chocolate, broken into squares**

$^{1}/_{2}$ cup whole milk

2 tbsp brandy

1 egg

2 egg yolks

1 tsp natural vanilla extract

10 fl oz/285 mL carton heavy cream

2 tbsp superfine sugar

4 tbsp strained yogurt

grated nutmeg to decorate

Method

1 Preheat the oven to 325°F/160°C/Gas Mark 3.
Place the chocolate, milk, and brandy in a
small saucepan. Cook over a low heat, stirring
occasionally, for 5–6 minutes, until just melted;
do not allow it to boil. Remove from the heat.

2 In a bowl, beat the egg, egg yolks, vanilla
extract, cream, and sugar until evenly
combined. Quickly add to the chocolate
mixture, mixing until smooth.

3 Divide the mixture evenly among 4 x
200 mL/7 fl oz ramekins. Place on a double
layer of newspaper in a roasting tin and pour
in just enough boiling water to reach halfway
up the sides of the dishes. Bake for 35–40
minutes until lightly set. Remove and leave to
cool for 30 minutes, then place in the
refrigerator for 1 hour. Top with the yogurt
and grated nutmeg to serve.

Serves 4

Red Berry and Banana Pie

Ingredients

12 pecan nuts, roughly chopped

12 oz/340 g all-purpose flour, sifted

3 tsp baking powder

**7 oz/200 g chilled butter, cubed, plus
extra for greasing**

4 ripe bananas

3 tbsp golden demerara sugar

4¹/₂ oz/125 g punnet raspberries

3 tbsp redcurrants or blackcurrants

Method

1 Finely grind the nuts in a food processor, or use a pestle and mortar. Put 1 tablespoon of the ground nuts, all the flour, and the baking powder into a bowl, then rub in the butter with your fingertips, until the mixture resembles fine breadcrumbs.

2 Remove and reserve a quarter of the mixture for the topping. Add 4–5 tablespoons of cold water to the remaining mixture and mix to a firm dough. Cover and refrigerate for 30 minutes.

3 Preheat the oven to 375°F/190°C/Gas Mark 5. Grease a 8 in/20 cm spring-form tin. Roll out the pastry on a lightly floured surface, then use it to line the tin. Line the pastry with baking paper and fill with baking beans. Bake for 15 minutes. Remove the paper and beans. Bake for a further 5 minutes until golden.

4 Slice the bananas into a bowl, stir in half the sugar, then fold in the berries. Spoon into the pastry case. Mix the reserved flour mixture with the rest of the sugar and the ground pecans, and sprinkle over the fruit. Bake for 15 minutes, then reduce the oven temperature to 350°F/180°C/Gas Mark 4 and bake for a further 15–20 minutes, until the top is golden. Cool for a few minutes before serving.

Serves 4

The sweet warmth of the fireside is comfort against the bitter cold of winter. What better way to while away the winter evenings than to cook delicious food. Some of the seasonal ingredients available in winter include citrus fruits, collard greens, leeks, papayas, potatoes, and winter squash. In this section you'll find recipes for hearty soups, including Spanish Pea Soup, and Tuscan Bean and Bread Soup; some warming casseroles, such as Chicken Rogan Josh; slow-cooked roasts; and baked desserts, including Date Puddings with Sticky Toffee Sauce and Rhubarb and Apple Crumble.

Winter

Winter Appetizers, Soups, & Snacks

Red Onion and Chili Tarts

Ingredients

13 oz/370 g pack ready-rolled puff pastry

1 tbsp olive oil

7 oz/200 g red onions, halved and finely sliced lengthways

1 small red chili, deseeded and thinly sliced

salt and black pepper

2 tbsp red pesto

1 oz/30 g pine nut kernels

Method

1 Preheat the oven to 425°F/220°C/Gas Mark 7. Open out the pastry sheet and cut out 4 x 4¼ in/12 cm rounds. Use a slightly smaller cutter or a sharp knife to score a ½ in/1 cm border on each; this will form the rim. Place the rounds on a baking sheet.

2 Heat the oil in a large frying pan. Fry the onions for 10 minutes or until softened, stirring. Add the chili and cook gently for 1 minute, then season.

3 Spread the pesto over the pastry rounds, leaving the rim clear. Spoon the onion mixture over the pesto and scatter with the pine nut kernels. Cook for 12–15 minutes, until the pastry has risen and is golden brown.

Serves 4

Spanish Pea Soup

Ingredients

2 cups dried green split peas

3 cups water

1 tbsp olive oil

1 tbsp Spanish paprika

2 onions, chopped

1 clove garlic, minced

1 green bell pepper, chopped

1 medium carrot, thinly sliced

**3 medium red potatoes, peeled
and diced**

8 cups chicken or vegetable bouillon

salt and pepper, to taste

2 ears fresh corn

$^1/_2$ bunch chives

low-fat yogurt to garnish (optional)

Method

1 Pick over the peas and rinse thoroughly. Place them in a large pot, cover with water, and bring to the boil. Simmer for 2 minutes, then remove from the heat, cover and let stand for 1 hour.

2 Meanwhile, heat oil in a large saucepan and add the paprika, chopped onion, and garlic. Sauté for 5 minutes or until the mixture is fragrant and the onions have softened. Add the green pepper, carrot, and cubed potato. Toss the vegetables thoroughly with the onion and paprika mixture until well coated, then continue to cook for 10 minutes, stirring continually.

3 Add the bouillon, peas, and salt and pepper to taste, then simmer, uncovered, for 2–3 hours, until the peas are very tender.

4 Cut the kernels off the corn cobs. Reserve $^1/_2$ cup of corn and add the remainder to the soup; simmer for 2 minutes. Purée the soup until thick and smooth, then serve with a few scattered corn kernels and some chopped chives. Garnish each plate with a teaspoon of yogurt if desired.

Serves 4

Turmeric-Infused Scallop Soup

Ingredients

2 tbsp unsalted butter

$^1/_2$ tsp turmeric

$2^1/_2$ lb/500 g prepared scallops

3 shallots, finely chopped

I bottle dry white wine

4 cups fish bouillon

$^1/_2$ cup crème fraiche

$3^1/_2$ cups heavy cream

**salt and freshly ground
   white pepper**

$^1/_2$ tsp white wine vinegar

Method

I   In a large saucepan, cook the butter, tumeric, scallops, and shallots over a moderately low heat, stirring, until the shallots are softened. Add the wine and bouillon and simmer the mixture until reduced by half. Remove from the heat and allow to cool.

2   Pour the soup into a blender, and blend until smooth. Pour the soup into a saucepan, and return to the heat. Add the crème fraiche and heavy cream and simmer, stirring occasionally, for 15 minutes.

3   Pour the soup through a fine sieve into a heatproof bowl. Stir in the white-pepper, vinegar, and salt to taste. In another bowl, whisk the remaining $^1/_2$ cup heavy cream until thickened and stir into the soup until incorporated..

Serves 10

Potato and Parsnip Puddings with Apple Sauce

Ingredients

12 oz/340 g potatoes, peeled and coarsely grated

5 oz/145 g parsnips, peeled and coarsely grated

1 onion, finely grated

1 tbsp finely chopped fresh sage or 1 tsp dried sage

1 medium egg, lightly beaten

4 tbsp dried breadcrumbs

salt and black pepper

2 tbsp olive oil

Sauce

11 oz/310 g cooking apples, peeled, cored, and chopped

grated zest and juice of ½ lemon

2 tbsp sugar or clear honey

1 tbsp finely chopped fresh sage or 1 tsp dried sage

3–4 tbsp sour cream (optional)

Method

1 To make the puddings, place the potatoes, parsnips, onion, sage, egg, breadcrumbs, and seasoning in a large bowl and mix together well. Cover and place in the refrigerator for 20 minutes.

2 Meanwhile, preheat the oven to 425°F/220°C/Gas Mark 7. To make the sauce, place the apples, lemon zest and juice, and the sugar or honey in a small, heavy-based saucepan with 2 tablespoons of water. Bring to the boil, cover, then reduce the heat and cook for 8–10 minutes, until the mixture forms a chunky purée. Remove from the heat and stir for 1 minute or until fluffy. Add the sage and sour cream, if using.

3 Brush 6 muffin tins with 1 tablespoon of the oil. Divide the pudding mixture among them, then brush the tops with half the remaining oil, and cook for 15 minutes. Remove from the oven, brush with the remaining oil, and cook for 5 minutes longer or until browned.

Serves 4

Tuscan Bean and Bread Soup

Ingredients

¹/₂ **loaf ciabatta**

3 tbsp olive oil

3 onions, chopped

3 cloves garlic, chopped

2 x 14 oz/400 g cans chopped tomatoes

14 oz/400 g can flageolet beans

2¹/₂ cups vegetable bouillon

salt and black pepper

fresh basil to garnish

Method

1 Preheat the oven to 300°F/150°C/Gas Mark 2. Cut the ciabatta into dice, then place in the oven for 10 minutes to dry out.

2 Heat the olive oil in a large saucepan, add the onions and garlic, and cook for 3–4 minutes, until soft. Add the tomatoes, beans, and bouillon, bring to the boil, then simmer for 2 minutes.

3 Stir in the diced ciabatta, bring the soup back to the boil, then simmer for a further 5 minutes. Season, then serve garnished with basil.

Serves 4

Baked Onions with Mushrooms and Pine Nuts

Ingredients

2 slices brown bread

4 large red onions

2 tbsp olive oil

2 cloves garlic, chopped

2 tbsp pine nut kernels

**7 oz/200 g mushrooms,
    finely chopped**

4 tbsp chopped fresh parsley

salt and black pepper

Method

1 Preheat the oven to 325°F/160°C/Gas Mark 3. Place the bread in the oven for 20 minutes or until it becomes crisp. Process in a food processor to make breadcrumbs. Alternatively, use a grater.

2 Meanwhile, slice the tops and bases off the onions. Place in a saucepan, cover with water, and bring to the boil. Cook for 10 minutes to soften. Drain, then leave to cool for 20 minutes.

3 Increase the oven temperature to 200°C/400°F/Gas Mark 6. Cut out the middle of each onion, leaving the shell intact, and finely chop. Heat the oil, then fry the garlic and chopped onion for 5 minutes. Add the pine nuts and mushrooms and fry for a further 5 minutes. Remove from the heat, then mix in the breadcrumbs, parsley, and seasoning. Fill the onion shells with the mixture, then wrap each onion in foil, leaving the tops open. Place on a baking sheet and cook for 40 minutes or until the onions are tender.

Serves 4

Mackerel Kebabs with Gooseberry Sauce

Ingredients

4 mackerel, about 13 oz/370 g
  each, filleted and cut into
  bite-sized pieces
olive oil for brushing

Sauce
1 oz/30 g butter
1 tbsp vegetable oil
1 onion, thinly sliced
1 bulb fennel, thinly sliced
6 oz/170 g gooseberries
1 oz/30 g sugar
salt and black pepper

Method

1 To make the sauce, heat the butter and oil in a saucepan and gently fry the onion and fennel, covered, for 10 minutes or until softened. Add the gooseberries and sugar and cook for 10 minutes or until the vegetables and gooseberries are tender. Season to taste.

2 Meanwhile, soak 8 wooden skewers in cold water for at least 10 minutes. Preheat the broiler to high, then thread the mackerel onto the skewers. Brush the fish with oil and season.

3 Broil the kebabs for 5 minutes, turning occasionally, until the fish flesh is opaque and the skin lightly charred. Serve with the sauce.

Serves 4

Spiced Pumpkin, Parsnip, and Pear Soup

Ingredients

3 lb/1 1/2 kg pumpkin of your choice

1 tbsp olive oil

1 lb/500 g parsnip, peeled and diced

2 small brown pears, peeled and diced

1 large red onion, chopped

3 cloves garlic, minced

1 tbsp curry powder

salt and pepper, to taste

6–8 cups vegetable or chicken bouillon

1/2 cup dry white wine

1/2 cup low-fat yogurt or buttermilk

1 bunch chives, snipped

Lentil Crisps

1/2 cup lentil flour

1/2 cup all-purpose flour

1/2 cup semolina flour

3/4 tsp curry powder

1/2 tsp salt

1/2 tsp pepper

2/3 cup warm water

olive oil spray

Method

1 Cut the pumpkin in half and place in a baking tray with 1/2 cup of water. Bake at 375°F/190°C/Gas Mark 5 for about 90 minutes or until the pumpkin is tender. Scoop out and discard the seeds, and peel away the skin.

2 Meanwhile, heat the olive oil in a large saucepan and add the diced parsnip, diced pears, chopped onion, garlic, curry powder, and salt and pepper to taste. Sauté, stirring occasionally, for about 20 minutes. Add the cooked pumpkin, bouillon, and white wine and bring to the boil. Simmer, uncovered, for about 40 minutes, then purée the soup until smooth. To serve, drizzle some yogurt or buttermilk over the soup and scatter the chives on top. Place a lentil crisp across each bowl.

3 To make the lentil crisps, preheat the oven to 425°F/220°C/Gas Mark 7. In a bowl, mix together all the dry ingredients, including the salt and pepper, and add enough of the water to form a kneadable dough. Knead well for 2 minutes, then roll out the dough as thinly as possible (a pasta machine works well here) to a rectangle of approximately 16in/40 cm x 6 in/15 cm. Using a knife or pizza cutter, cut the dough into long, thin triangles and place these on a non-stick oven tray. Spray with olive oil, add salt if desired, and bake for 10 minutes, until crisp and golden. Cool on a wire rack. Repeat with the remaining dough.

Serves 4

Curried Cream of Vegetable Soup

Ingredients

3 tbsp groundnut or vegetable oil

2 tbsp curry powder

pinch each of ground cinnamon,
  nutmeg, turmeric and ginger

3 carrots, diced

2 onions, chopped

2 cloves garlic, chopped

2 potatoes, diced

2 zucchinis, diced

4 cups vegetable bouillon

10 oz/285 g can cannellini beans, drained

8 oz/225 g can red kidney beans, drained

7 fl oz/200 mL tub crème fraîche

salt

2 tsp chopped fresh Italian
  parsley to garnish

Method

1 Place the oil in a large heavy-based saucepan. Add the curry powder, cinnamon, nutmeg, turmeric, and ginger and cook for 1 minute, then add the carrots, onions, garlic, potatoes, and zucchinis. Stir to coat thoroughly in the oil and spice mixture, and cook for a further 5 minutes.

2 Add the bouillon and bring to the boil. Reduce the heat and simmer for 20 minutes or until the vegetables are tender. Add the cannellini and red kidney beans and gently heat through. Remove from the heat and stir in the crème fraîche. Season to taste and serve sprinkled with the parsley.

Serves 4

Salmon and Rice Noodle Soup

Ingredients

2 stalks lemon grass

2 cloves garlic, chopped

1 large onion, chopped

1 tsp turmeric

1 tsp hot chili powder

1 tbsp vegetable oil

14 fl oz/400 mL can coconut milk

1¼ cups fish or chicken bouillon

8 oz/225 g skinless salmon fillet,
 cut into 1 in/2½ cm cubes

salt

4 oz/115 g rice noodles

7 oz/200 g pack fresh bean sprouts

fresh cilantro to garnish

1 lime, quartered, to serve

Method

1 Peel the outer layers from the lemon grass stalks and finely chop the lower white bulbous parts, discarding the fibrous tops. Blend to a chunky paste with the garlic, onion, turmeric, and chili powder in a food processor, or grind with a pestle and mortar.

2 Heat the oil in a large, heavy-based saucepan. Fry the paste for 5 minutes to release its flavors, stirring often. Mix in the coconut milk and bouillon, bring to the boil, stirring, then reduce the heat, cover, and simmer for 15 minutes. Add the salmon and salt to taste, then simmer, covered, for 5 minutes or until the fish has cooked through.

3 Meanwhile, prepare the rice noodles according to the packet instructions. Drain and rinse with cold water. Place the bean sprouts in a saucepan of boiling water, cook for 1 minute, then drain. Divide the rice noodles and bean sprouts among serving bowls and ladle the salmon and coconut soup over the top. Garnish with cilantro and serve with the lime.

Serves 4

Winter Casserole Cooking

Seafood Casserole

Ingredients

1 tbsp olive oil

1 medium onion, roughly chopped

1 leek, finely chopped

2 cloves garlic, crushed

2 cups canned tomatoes

2 bay leaves

1 tbsp parsley, chopped

1/4 cup dry white wine

salt and freshly ground black pepper

2 lb/900 g assorted fish and seafood

2 tbsp fresh oregano, chopped

Method

1 Heat the oil in a flame proof casserole dish. Sauté the onion, leek, and garlic until softened and slightly golden.

2 Add the tomatoes, bay leaves, parsley, wine, salt, and pepper. Bring to the boil, cover, and simmer gently for 20 minutes.

3 Stir in any firm-fleshed fish and simmer for 5 minutes. Stir in the remaining soft-fleshed fish, placing the shellfish on the top.

4 Cover with a lid and continue cooking for 5–7 minutes until the fish is tender, and the shellfish have opened. Discard any that remain closed.

5 Serve garnished with the oregano.

Serves 4

Lamb Shanks with Root Vegetables

Ingredients

2 tablespoons olive oil

2 parsnips, peeled and cut into large chunks

1 medium sweet potato, peeled, and cut into large chunks

1 yellow turnips, peeled and cut into large chunks

1 bunch scallions, trimmed

2 tablespoons olive oil, extra

2 cloves garlic, crushed

4 lamb shanks

³/₄ cup beef bouillon

¹/₄ cup water

¹/₂ cup red wine

1 tbsp tomato paste

2 sprigs rosemary, chopped

bouquet garni

freshly ground pepper and salt

Method

1 Heat 1 tablespoon of the oil in a large heavy-based saucepan, add the root vegetables, and cook quickly until brown. Set aside on a plate. Add the extra oil to the pan and brown the garlic and lamb for a few minutes.

2 To the pan, add the bouillon, water, red wine, tomato paste, rosemary, bouquet garni, pepper, and salt. Bring to the boil, reduce the heat, and leave to simmer, with the lid on, for 20 minutes.

3 Return the vegetables to the pan and continue to cook for another 30 minutes or until everything is cooked.

4 Before serving, remove the bouquet garni and check the seasoning.

Serves 4

Lamb and Apricot Casserole

Ingredients

1 tbsp sunflower oil

1 lb/455 g lean boneless lamb leg
  or fillet, cut into 1 in/2 cm cubes

1 large onion, chopped

1 clove garlic, finely chopped

2 tbsp all-purpose flour

1 tsp ground cilantro

1 tsp ground cumin

1 1/2 cups vegetable bouillon

1/2 cup red wine

1 cup baby button mushrooms

1 tbsp tomato paste

1 bouquet garni

freshly ground black pepper

1 1/2 cups dried apricots

2 tbsp chopped fresh cilantro,
  plus extra leaves to garnish

Method

1 Preheat the oven to 160°C/325°F/Gas Mark 3. Heat the oil in a flame- and ovenproof casserole dish on the hotplate. Add the lamb and cook for about 5 minutes or until browned. Remove and keep warm.

2 Add the onion and garlic to the juices in the dish and cook for 5 minutes or until softened. Return the lamb to the dish with the flour, ground cilantro, and cumin and cook for 1 minute, stirring. Slowly add the bouillon and wine and bring to the boil, stirring. Stir in the mushrooms, tomato paste, bouquet garni, and pepper. Cover and cook in the oven for 1 hour.

3 Stir in the apricots and cook for a further 30 minutes or until the lamb is tender. Remove and discard the bouquet garni, stir in the chopped cilantro, then garnish with more fresh cilantro.

Serves 4

Lamb Shanks with Fava Beans, Olives, and Risoni

Ingredients

2 tbsp olive oil

2 cloves garlic, crushed

4 lamb shanks

1 onion, chopped

2 cups beef bouillon

4 sprigs oregano

2 tbsp tomato paste

2 cups water

1 cup rice

1 cup fava beans

¹/₂ cup olives

2 tsp fresh oregano, chopped

salt and freshly ground pepper

Method

1 Heat the oil in a large saucepan, add the garlic, lamb shanks, and onion, and cook for 5 minutes or until the shanks are lightly browned.

2 Add the bouillon, oregano sprigs, tomato paste, and half the water. Bring to the boil, reduce the heat, and leave to simmer, covered for 40 minutes.

3 Remove the shanks, slice the meat off the bone, and set aside.

4 Add the rice and the remaining water, cook for a further 5 minutes, then add the fava beans, olives, meat, oregano, salt, and pepper. Cook for 5 minutes more and serve.

Serves 4

Lamb Osso Bucco

Ingredients

2 tbsp all-purpose flour

salt and black pepper

4 lamb leg shanks, trimmed of excess fat

2 tbsp olive oil

1 onion, finely chopped

1 carrot, finely chopped

1 stick celery, finely chopped

**2 cups canned chopped tomatoes
   with garlic and herbs**

1 tbsp sun-dried tomato paste

$^1/_2$ cup dry white wine

2 cups lamb bouillon

Garnish

1 tbsp chopped fresh parsley

1 tbsp chopped fresh mint

finely grated zest of 1 lemon

1 clove garlic, finely chopped

Method

1 Preheat the oven to 160°C/325°F/Gas Mark 3. Mix together the flour, salt, and pepper on a plate. Dip the lamb pieces into the mixture to coat well. Heat 1 tablespoon of the oil in a large heavy-based frying pan until hot but not smoking. Add the coated lamb and cook over a medium to high heat for 5–8 minutes, turning frequently, until browned on all sides. Transfer to a deep ovenproof dish.

2 Heat the remaining oil in the pan, add the onion, carrot, and celery and cook over a low heat for 4–5 minutes, until softened. Add the tomatoes, tomato paste, wine and bouillon and bring to the boil, stirring occasionally. Pour over the lamb, cover with foil, and bake for 1$^3/_4$–2 hours, until the meat is tender, turning it over halfway through. Season to taste.

3 To make the garnish, mix together the parsley, mint, lemon zest, and garlic. Sprinkle the garnish over the lamb and serve.

Serves 4

Beef Braised in Rioja

Ingredients

3 tbsp olive oil

1 1/2 lb/680 g stewing beef, trimmed
of fat and cut into 2 1/2 in/6 cm chunks

6 shallots, finely chopped

2 cloves garlic, crushed

2 sticks celery, thickly sliced

1 1/2 cups mushrooms, thickly sliced

1/2 tsp ground allspice

1/2 bottle full-bodied red wine

1 cup tomato purée

2 sprigs fresh thyme

salt and black pepper

Method

1 Preheat the oven to 180°C/350°F/Gas Mark 4. Heat the oil in a flameproof casserole dish or a large saucepan and fry the meat over a high heat, stirring, for 5–10 minutes, until browned. Remove from the pan, then add the shallots, garlic, and celery. Cook, stirring, for 3–4 minutes, until lightly browned.

2 Add the mushrooms and cook for 1 minute or until softened. Stir in the allspice, wine, tomato purée, 1 sprig of thyme, and seasoning. Return the meat to the dish or pan and bring the mixture to a simmer.

3 Cover and cook in the oven or over a low heat on the hotplate for 1 1/2–2 hours, until the beef is tender. Season again if necessary, then serve garnished with the remaining thyme.

Serves 4

Beef Carbonade

Ingredients

2–3 tbsp vegetable oil

2 lb/900 g braising or stewing steak, cut into 1 in/2 cm cubes

1 large onion, thinly sliced

1 tbsp all-purpose flour

2 tbsp soft dark brown sugar

1 can Guinness

2 cups beef bouillon

1 tbsp tomato paste

1 bouquet garni

salt and black pepper

fresh parsley to garnish

Method

1 Preheat the oven to 160°C/325°F/Gas Mark 3. Heat 2 tablespoons of the oil in a flameproof casserole dish. Add one-third of the beef and fry over a high heat for 6–7 minutes, turning until browned on all sides. Remove from the pan while you cook the remaining batches, adding more oil if necessary. Set the beef aside.

2 Lower the heat, add the onion, and cook for 5 minutes, stirring. Sprinkle in the flour and sugar and stir for 1–2 minutes. Pour in the Guiness and bouillon and bring to the boil, stirring. Return the beef to the dish and add the tomato paste and bouquet garni. Season and stir well, then cover.

3 Transfer the dish to the oven and cook for 1½–2 hours, until the beef is tender and cooked through. Stir 2–3 times during cooking, adding a little water if necessary. Discard the bouquet garni and season again if necessary. Garnish with the parsley.

Serves 10

Rabbit, Olive, and Onion Casserole

Ingredients

1 1/2 lb/680 g rabbit portions

2 cups dry white wine

3 sprigs fresh oregano

3 bay leaves

5 tbsp olive oil

1 cup baby onions, peeled and halved

6 cloves garlic, unpeeled

1 tbsp paprika

2/3 cup chicken bouillon

1/2 cup black olives

salt and freshly ground black pepper

fresh oregano sprigs to garnish

crusty bread to serve

Method

1 In a large bowl, combine the rabbit, wine, oregano, and bay leaves. Cover and refrigerate overnight.

2 Drain the rabbit and reserve the marinade. Preheat the oven to 180°C/350°F/Gas Mark 4.

3 Heat the oil in a large frying pan and brown the rabbit, a few pieces at a time, on both sides. Remove the rabbit and place it in a casserole dish.

4 Brown the onions and garlic in the pan. Once the onions are golden, add the paprika. Stir continuously for 2 minutes, then add the bouillon and reserved marinade. Bring to the boil.

5 Pour the onion and bouillon mixture over the rabbit, add the olives, and season with salt and pepper.

6 Cover and bake for 1 1/4 hours or until the rabbit is cooked and tender. Garnish with fresh oregano sprigs and serve with plenty of the bread to mop up the juices.

Serves 4

Chicken Rogan Josh

Ingredients

8 skinless boneless chicken thighs

1 tbsp vegetable oil

1 small red and 1 small green bell pepper, deseeded and thinly sliced

1 onion, thinly sliced

2 in/5 cm piece of fresh root ginger, finely chopped

2 cloves garlic, crushed

2 tbsp garam masala

1 tsp each paprika, turmeric, and chili powder

4 cardamom pods, crushed

salt

1 cup plain yogurt

2 cups canned chopped tomatoes

fresh cilantro to garnish

Method

1 Cut each chicken thigh into 4 pieces. Heat the oil in a large heavy-based frying pan and add the bell peppers, onion, ginger, garlic, spices, and a good pinch of salt. Fry over a low heat for 5 minutes or until the bell peppers and onion have softened.

2 Add the chicken and 2 tablespoons of the yogurt. Increase the heat to medium and cook for 4 minutes or until the yogurt is absorbed. Repeat with the rest of the yogurt.

3 Increase the heat to high, stir in the tomatoes and 1 cup of water, and bring to the boil. Reduce the heat, cover and simmer for 30 minutes or until the chicken is tender, stirring occasionally and adding more water if the sauce becomes too dry.

4 Uncover the pan, increase the heat to high, and cook, stirring constantly, for 5 minutes or until the sauce thickens. Garnish with the cilantro.

Serves 4

Winter Roast Cooking

Roasted Shallots with Rosemary

Ingredients

1 1/4 lb/570 g shallots or pickling onions

2 tbsp olive oil

1–2 tbsp chopped fresh rosemary

black pepper

Method

1 Preheat the oven to 400°F/200°C/Gas Mark 6. Place the shallots in a roasting tin, drizzle over the oil, sprinkle with the rosemary and black pepper, then toss to mix well.

2 Cook in the oven for 30–40 minutes, until the shallots are tender and golden brown, stirring once or twice. Serve hot.

Serves 10

Roast Partridge with Bacon and Sage

Ingredients

1 lemon, quartered

16 fresh sage leaves, plus extra to garnish, or 2 tsp dried sage

4 oven-ready partridges

salt and black pepper

8 strips thinly sliced dry-cured bacon

2 tbsp olive oil

1 cup chicken bouillon

4 tbsp red or white wine

2 tsp redcurrant jelly

1–2 tsp balsamic vinegar

$^{1}/_{2}$ oz/15 g chilled butter, cubed

Method

1 Preheat the oven to 425°F/220°C/Gas Mark 7. Place a lemon quarter and 2 sage leaves or a sprinkling of dried sage in each bird. Season well, then wrap in 2 strips of bacon, tucking in 2 more sage leaves or a little more dried sage. Place in a roasting tin and drizzle with the oil. Roast, uncovered, for 30–35 minutes, basting once or twice, until tender and cooked. Remove the birds and keep warm.

2 Pour the cooking juices into a saucepan and add the bouillon and wine. Boil rapidly, stirring all the time, for 7 minutes or until reduced by half. Add 1 teaspoon of the redcurrant jelly and boil again for 1–2 minutes. Stir in the rest of the redcurrant jelly, the vinegar, and the seasoning to taste.

3 Remove the pan from the heat and stir in the butter until melted. Serve the sauce with the partridges, garnished with sage leaves, if using.

Serves 4

Glazed Scotch Fillet with Tomato Potato Wedges

Ingredients

3 lb/1¼ kg piece of scotch fillet

salt and pepper

2 tsp olive oil

5 medium-sized potatoes

1 tsp crushed garlic

2 tbsp sun-dried tomato pesto

1 tbsp water

1 tbsp olive oil extra

Herbed Wine Marinade

¼ cup soy sauce

2 tbsp brown sugar

¼ tsp ground ginger

2 tbsp wine vinegar

1 clove garlic, crushed

2 tbsp tomato ketchup

Method

1 Rub the salt, pepper, and 2 teaspoons of oil all over the meat and tie with kitchen string at 1 in/2½ cm intervals, to keep in shape. Mix all the marinade ingredients together and set aside.

2 Peel and halve the potatoes, then cut each half into 4–6 wedges. Rinse the potato wedges well, drain, and place in a large bowl. Mix the garlic, tomato pesto, water, and extra oil together. Pour this mixture over the wedges and turn to coat well. Place in a large aluminum foil dish, in a single layer if possible. Set aside.

3 Place the roast in a foil baking dish, brush with marinade and cook in oven at 400°F/200°C/Gas Mark 6 Brush with marinade every 10 minutes without turning, then turn the meat after 40 minutes and continue to brush with marinade at 10 minute intervals, until meat is cooked; about 75 minutes for rare, 90 minutes for medium and 90 minutes for well done.

4 When the meat has been half cooked place the potatoes in the oven, turn the wedges over after about 20 minutes, they should be ready for serving at the same time as the meat.

5 When cooked, stand the roast, covered with kitchen foil, for 10 minutes before carving. Carve and serve with the tomato potato wedges and vegetables or salad of choice.

Serves 8–10

Mediterranean Roast Lamb

Ingredients

¹/₂ leg of lamb, about 3¹/₃ lb/1¹/₂ kg

4 cloves garlic, cut into slivers

several sprigs of fresh rosemary,
   cut into pieces

4 tbsp olive oil

salt and black pepper

3 large bell peppers (red, green,
   and yellow), deseeded and
   cut into large pieces

3 large zucchinis, cut into
   large chunks

1²/₃ lb/750 g small new potatoes,
   unpeeled

8 oz/225 g cherry tomatoes

Method

1 Preheat the oven to 375°F/190°C/Gas Mark 5. Make several incisions in the top of the lamb with a sharp knife and push in two-thirds of the garlic slivers and rosemary. Drizzle with 1 tablespoon of the oil and season.

2 Meanwhile, place the peppers, zucchinis, and potatoes in a large roasting tin and season. Stir in the remaining garlic, rosemary, and oil, then set aside. Put the lamb on a rack in another roasting tin, and roast near the top of the oven for 40 minutes.

3 Place the marinated vegetables in the oven, on a shelf below the lamb, and turn the meat over. Roast for 25 minutes, then add the tomatoes to the vegetables. Roast for a further 10 minutes or until the lamb is cooked. Remove the lamb from the oven, cover with kitchen foil and leave to rest for 10 minutes. Cook the vegetables for a further 10 minutes, turning once. Serve the lamb with the vegetables.

Serves 4

Winter Mains

Liver with Red Grapes

Ingredients

1–2 tbsp all-purpose flour

salt and black pepper

1 lb/455 g thinly sliced lamb
   or calf liver

2 tbsp groundnut oil

1 oz/30 g butter

1 tbsp soft light or dark
   brown sugar

2 tbsp raspberry or red
   wine vinegar

1 cup chicken bouillon

5 oz/145 g seedless red or black grapes,
   halved if large

fresh Italian parsley to garnish

Method

1 Mix together the flour, salt, and pepper on a plate. Dip the liver into the mixture to coat well. Heat the oil in a large heavy-based frying pan, add half the liver, and cook for 2–3 minutes on each side, until cooked through. Remove from the pan and cook the remaining liver, then set aside.

2 Melt the butter in the pan until foaming, then stir in the sugar. Add the vinegar, stir vigorously, then add the bouillon and bring to the boil.

3 Lower the heat, add the grapes, and simmer for 4–5 minutes. Return the liver to the pan and reheat for 1–2 minutes, shaking the pan and spooning the sauce over the liver. Garnish with the parsley.

Serves 4

Venison Steaks with Parsnips and Horseradish

Ingredients

7 tbsp olive oil

1 tbsp balsamic vinegar

4 tbsp port

1 tsp juniper berries, crushed

1 onion, sliced

2 x venison steaks 12 oz/340 g each

salt and black pepper

1/2 cup chicken or beef bouillon

1 tsp redcurrant jelly

4 large parsnips, cut into wedges

Horseradish Cream

1 tsp traditional hot horseradish

1 tsp chopped fresh tarragon

5 tbsp crème fraîche

Method

1 Mix 2 tablespoons of the oil with the vinegar, port, and juniper berries. Put the onion and venison into a shallow non-metallic dish, season, then pour the marinade over. Cover and refrigerate for 4 hours or overnight, turning once. Drain the venison on kitchen paper towel. Reserve the marinade.

2 Heat 1 tablespoon of oil in a large heavy-based frying pan, then fry the steaks for 4–5 minutes, until browned. Turn over and cook for 3–4 minutes more. Remove and keep warm. Strain the marinade and add with the bouillon to the pan along with the bouillon. Boil for 3–4 minutes, until reduced by half. Stir in the redcurrant jelly and cook for 2 minutes. Season.

3 Meanwhile, preheat the broiler to medium. Place the parsnips on a baking tray and brush with 2 tablespoons of the oil. Season and broil for 5–6 minutes, then turn, brush with the remaining oil, and cook for a further 5 minutes or until golden. To make the horseradish cream, mix together the horseradish, tarragon, and crème fraîche. Serve with the venison, parsnips, and redcurrant sauce.

Serves 4

Creamy Chicken Korma

Ingredients

3 tbsp vegetable oil

1 onion, chopped

2 cloves garlic, crushed

3 tbsp all-purpose flour

2 tbsp mild korma curry powder

1²/₃ lb/750 g skinless boneless chicken breasts, cut into 1 in/2¹/₂ cm cubes

1¹/₃ cups chicken bouillon

1 oz/30 g raisins

1 tbsp chopped fresh cilantro

1 tsp garam masala

juice of ¹/₂ lemon

4 tbsp sour cream

Method

1 Heat the oil in a large heavy-based saucepan, add the onion and garlic, and cook gently for 5 minutes or until softened.

2 Put the flour and curry powder into a bowl and mix together. Toss the chicken in the seasoned flour, coating well. Reserve the flour. Add the chicken to the onion and garlic, then cook, stirring, for 3-4 minutes, until lightly browned. Stir in the seasoned flour and cook for 1 minute.

3 Add the bouillon and raisins and bring to the boil, stirring. Cover and simmer for 15 minutes. Add the cilantro and garam masala and cook for a further 5 minutes or until the flavors are released and the chicken is cooked through. Remove the pan from the heat and stir in the lemon juice and sour cream. Return to the heat and warm through, taking care not to let the mixture boil.

Serves 4

Honey-Glazed Chicken with Goat's Cheese

Ingredients

4 skinless boneless chicken breasts

3¹/₂ oz/100 g soft goat's cheese

4 sprigs fresh thyme, plus

1 tsp chopped fresh thyme

2 tbsp clear honey

salt and black pepper

¹/₂ tsp paprika, plus extra

to garnish

2 yellow bell peppers and 2 red bell

peppers, deseeded and thickly sliced

1 red onion, thickly sliced

2 tbsp olive oil

Method

1 Preheat the broiler to high. Use a sharp knife to cut a deep slit in the side of each chicken breast, opening it out to form a pocket. Spoon the goat's cheese into the pockets and add a sprig of thyme to each. Fold the chicken over to enclose the cheese and secure the edges with wetted cocktail sticks.

2 Place the chicken breasts on a baking sheet and brush with the honey. Season, then sprinkle with paprika. Broil for 7–8 minutes, until golden brown. Turn and cook the other side for a further 7–8 minutes, until tender and cooked through. Remove the cocktail sticks.

3 Meanwhile, toss the peppers and onion in the oil. Heat a ridged cast-iron griddle pan and cook the vegetables for 3–4 minutes, until golden, turning once. Alternatively, cook under a preheated broiler for the same time. Sprinkle with the chopped thyme, spoon onto plates, and top with the chicken breasts. Sprinkle with a little paprika.

Serves 4

Gnocchi with Pork and Peppers

Ingredients

12 oz/340 g pork steak, cubed

4 cloves garlic, very finely chopped

1 tbsp dried oregano

juice of ¹/₂ lemon

6 tbsp extra virgin olive oil

salt and black pepper

2 tbsp very finely chopped onion

1 tbsp very finely chopped celery

3 tbsp very finely chopped
fresh parsley

9 oz/255 g yellow bell peppers, deseeded
and cut into 1 in/2¹/₂ cm pieces

1 cup tomato puree

3 tbsp beef bouillon

2 x 14 oz/400 g packs potato gnocchi

1 oz/30 g black olives, pitted and
cut into strips

Method

1 Place the pork in a shallow, non-metallic dish and mix in half the garlic, the oregano, lemon juice, 1 tablespoon of the oil, and the seasoning. Cover and place in the refrigerator to marinate for 1 hour.

2 Heat the remaining oil in a large heavy-based saucepan. Add the onion and a pinch of salt and fry for 5 minutes or until softened. Stir in the remaining garlic, celery, parsley, and peppers and cook over a low heat for 10 minutes or until the peppers begin to soften.

3 Mix in the tomato purée and simmer for 10 minutes, stirring often. Add the pork, its marinade, and the bouillon. Simmer, uncovered, for 10 minutes or until the sauce has thickened and the pork is cooked, stirring occasionally.

4 Meanwhile, cook the gnocchi in plenty of boiling salted water until tender but still firm to the bite. Drain and transfer to a warmed bowl. Spoon the sauce over and toss, then scatter the olives over.

Serves 4

Tomato, Parsley, and Cheese Pie

Ingredients

6 oz/170 g all-purpose flour

pinch of salt

3 oz/85 g matured Cheddar cheese, grated

1 tbsp grated Parmesan cheese

3 egg yolks

3 oz/85 g butter, softened

3 tomatoes, skinned and sliced

2 tbsp each chopped parsley, basil, and thyme

2 oz/55 g Emmenthal cheese, sliced

Method

1 Sift the flour and salt onto a board. Make a well in the center, add the cheeses, egg yolks, and butter, and gradually work into the flour. Knead until smooth, form into a ball, cover, and chill for 1 hour.

2 Roll out the dough and use to line 8 x 3 in/7 $^1/_2$ cm tartlet tins or one 9 in/23 cm tin. Chill for 20 minutes. Bake blind (lined with waxed paper and filled with dried beans) in a preheated 400°F/200°C/Gas Mark 6 for 20 minutes. Take out, remove the waxed paper and dried beans, and return to the oven for 5 minutes.

3 Layer the tomato slices in the pastry case or cases, sprinkling each layer with the herbs. Top with the Emmenthal cheese. Return to the oven for 5 minutes or until the cheese is bubbling. Leave to cool in the tins. Serve at room temperature.

Serves 4

305

Baked Monk Fish with Hazelnut Crumb Topping

Ingredients

2 small oranges

1 small bulb fennel, thinly sliced

2 tablespoons olive oil, plus extra
   for greasing

4 pieces monk fish fillet, about
   5 oz/145 g each

salt and black pepper

2 tbsp snipped fresh chives

2 oz/55 g whole blanched
   hazelnuts, chopped

2 oz/55 g fresh brown breadcrumbs

Method

1 Preheat the oven to 400°F/200°C/Gas Mark 6. Finely grate the zest and squeeze the juice from 1 orange. Slice the top and bottom off the remaining orange, then cut away the peel and pith, following the curve of the fruit. Cut between the membranes to release the segments, then chop the flesh.

2 Arrange the fennel and orange slices in a lightly greased shallow ovenproof dish and place the fish on top. Sprinkle with the orange juice and season.

3 Mix the chives with the orange rind, hazelnuts, breadcrumbs, and oil, season well, and stir to mix evenly. Spoon the breadcrumb mixture over the fish, smoothing to cover. Cook in the oven for 35–40 minutes, until the fish is cooked through and the topping is golden brown.

Serves 4

Mediterranean Fish Stew with Rouille

Ingredients

2¹/₄ lb/I kg mixed fish and shellfish,
such as cod, red mullet, or mackerel
fillet, raw shell-on large shrimps and
prepared squid

I lb/500 g Irish cooked mussels
in garlic butter sauce

2 tbsp olive oil

I onion, finely chopped

I tsp fennel seeds

7 fl oz/200 mL dry white wine

14 oz/400 g can chopped tomatoes

salt and black pepper

Rouille

2 cloves garlic, chopped

I small red chili, deseeded and chopped

3 tbsp chopped fresh cilantro

salt and black pepper

3 tbsp mayonnaise

I tbsp olive oil

Method

1 First make the rouille. Crush together the garlic, chili and cilantro with a pinch of salt in a pestle and mortar. Stir in the mayonnaise and oil, mix well, and season to taste. Refrigerate until needed.

2 Skin the fish, if necessary, and cut into 2 in/5 cm chunks. Shell the shrimps, then slit open the back of each one and scrape out any black vein. Rinse well. Cut the squid into 2 in/5 cm rings. Shell the mussels, reserving a few with shells on to garnish.

3 Heat the oil in a large heavy-based saucepan and fry the onion for 4 minutes, to soften. Add the fennel seeds and fry for another minute, then add the wine, tomatoes, and seasoning. Bring to the boil, then simmer, uncovered, for 5 minutes, until slightly thickened. Add the fish, squid, and shrimps and simmer, covered, for a further 5–6 minutes, stirring occasionally, until the shrimps are pink and everything is cooked. Add all the mussels and heat through. Season and serve with the rouille.

Serves 4

Pasta with Roasted Squash and Sage Butter

Ingredients

2 tbsp olive oil

2 cloves garlic, chopped

2 tbsp chopped fresh sage
plus extra sprigs to garnish,
or 2 tsp dried sage

1 butternut squash, peeled, deseeded
and cut into $^1/_2$ in/1 cm dice

12 oz/340 g dried pasta quills

salt and black pepper

3 oz/85 g butter

1 oz/30 g pine nut kernels

1 oz/30 g Parmesan cheese, grated

Method

1 Preheat the oven to 450°F/230°C/Gas Mark 8. Toss together the oil, garlic, 1 tablespoon of the chopped fresh sage or 1 teaspoon of the dried sage, and the butternut squash. Cook at the top of the oven for 20 minutes or until tender.

2 Meanwhile, cook the pasta in plenty of boiling salted water, according to the packet instructions, until tender but still firm to the bite.

3 Melt the butter in a large frying pan, add the remaining chopped sage or dried sage, and fry gently for 2–3 minutes. Meanwhile, heat another frying pan and dry-fry the pine nut kernels for 3–4 minutes over a high heat, until golden.

4 Drain the pasta, reserving 4 tablespoons of the cooking liquid. Add the reserved cooking liquid to the butter, then add the pasta and cooked squash. Toss, then serve sprinkled with the Parmesan, pine nuts, and pepper. Garnish with the fresh sage, if using.

Serves 4

Breaded Lamb Chops with Mash

Ingredients

2 tsp Dijon mustard

2 tsp clear honey

2 cloves garlic, crushed

**I tbsp chopped fresh rosemary,
    plus extra sprigs to garnish**

3 tbsp olive oil or melted butter

salt and black pepper

8 lamb loin chops

**3¹/₂ oz/100 g fine white fresh
    breadcrumbs**

Parsnip Mash

I lb/455 g parsnips, cut into chunks

**I lb/455 g floury potatoes, such as
    King Edward, cut into chunks**

2 cloves garlic

2 oz/55 g butter

5 tbsp light cream

freshly grated nutmeg

Method

I Mix together the mustard, honey, garlic, rosemary, and 2 tablespoons of the oil or butter. Season well with pepper. Thickly brush the mixture all over the chops, then coat with the breadcrumbs.

2 To make the mash, cook the parsnips, potatoes, and garlic in a saucepan of boiling salted water for 15–20 minutes, until tender. Drain well, then mash with the butter and cream until smooth. Season with salt, pepper, and nutmeg.

3 Meanwhile, preheat the broilerl to medium-high. Place the chops on the broiler rack and drizzle with the remaining oil or butter. Broil for 7–8 minutes on each side, until tender; adjust the heat, if necessary, to ensure that the breadcrumbs don't burn. Serve the chops with the mash and garnish with rosemary.

Serves 4

Lamb with Mint Butter and Saffron Mash

Ingredients

2 lb/900 g floury potatoes, such as
   Desirée or King Edward,
   cut into chunks
salt and black pepper
3 oz/85 g butter, softened
2 tbsp chopped fresh mint,
   plus extra leaves to garnish
$^1/_2$ tsp ground cumin
4 tbsp light cream
pinch of saffron strands
4 lamb leg steaks, about
   11 oz/310 g each

Method

1 Cook the potatoes in a large saucepan of lightly salted water for 15 minutes or until tender. Meanwhile, mash together 1 $^1/_2$ oz/45 g of the butter, the mint, cumin, and a little pepper, then cover and refrigerate. Put the cream and saffron strands in a small saucepan, gently heat through, then remove from the heat and set aside for 5 minutes to infuse.

2 Preheat the broiler to high. Season the lamb steaks and broil for 4–5 minutes on each side, or until cooked to your liking. Cover with kitchen foil and leave to rest for 5 minutes. Meanwhile, drain the potatoes well and mash with a potato masher. Mix in the remaining butter and the saffron cream, and season.

3 Divide the chilled mint butter among the steaks and broil for a few seconds until the butter melts. Serve the steaks with the saffron mash and any pan juices. Garnish with mint.

Serves 4

Mixed Vegetable Cheese Bake

Ingredients

1 large butternut squash, peeled, deseeded, and cut into chunks

salt and black pepper

3 tbsp olive oil

1 large cauliflower, cut into florets

12 oz/340 g mushrooms, sliced

2 tbsp fresh white breadcrumbs

2 tbsp freshly grated Parmesan cheese

Sauce

1 oz/30 g butter, plus extra for greasing

1 oz/30 g all-purpose flour

pinch of cayenne pepper

1 cup whole milk

1 tsp English mustard

3½ oz/100 g Cheddar, grated

Method

1 Preheat the oven to 400°F/200°C/Gas Mark 6. Put the squash into an ovenproof dish, season, then drizzle half the oil over the squash. Roast for 25 minutes, stirring once, until tender. Meanwhile, cook the cauliflower in boiling salted water for 5 minutes or until just tender. Drain, reserving 7 fl oz/200 mL of the cooking water, then refresh in cold water and set aside. Fry the mushrooms in the remaining oil for 4–5 minutes.

2 To make the sauce, melt the butter in a saucepan and stir in the flour and cayenne pepper. Cook for 2 minutes, then gradually stir in the reserved cooking liquid. Cook for 2–3 minutes, until thick, then gradually stir in the milk. Simmer, stirring, for 10 minutes. Remove from the heat, then stir in the mustard and the cheese, until melted. Season to taste.

3 Reduce the oven temperature to 350°F/180°C/Gas Mark 4. Add the cauliflower to the squash, then divide among 4 individual ovenproof dishes. Scatter the mushrooms on top and pour the sauce over. Mix the breadcrumbs and Parmesan, then sprinkle over each dish. Bake for 30–35 minutes.

Serves 4

Pork Steaks with Mushroom Sauce

Ingredients

1 tbsp vegetable oil

**4 pork shoulder steaks, trimmed
  of excess fat**

black pepper

**chopped fresh parsley
  to garnish**

Sauce

**12 oz/340 g closed-cup
  mushrooms, sliced**

1 clove garlic, crushed

1 tsp paprika

1 cup beef bouillon

1 tbsp redcurrant jelly

1 tbsp tomato paste

2 tsp cornstarch

2 tbsp low-fat crème fraîche

Method

1 Heat the oil in a large frying pan. Season the pork steaks with pepper and fry for 1 minute on each side to brown, then cook for a further 5 minutes on each side or until tender and cooked through. Remove and keep warm.

2 To make the sauce, add the mushrooms and garlic to the frying pan and fry for 2 minutes or until softened. Stir in the paprika, beef bouillon, redcurrant jelly, and tomato paste. Bring to the boil, then simmer for 5 minutes or until reduced slightly.

3 Mix the cornstarch with 1 tablespoon of water to form a paste, stir into the sauce, and simmer for a further 2 minutes or until the sauce has thickened.

4 Return the pork steaks to the pan, turn off the heat, and stir in the crème fraîche. Season to taste and serve garnished with the parsley.

Serves 4

Winter Desserts

Warm Apricot Brioches

Ingredients

4 individual brioches

6 fresh apricots, halved and stoned,
   or 12 canned apricot halves, drained

6 tbsp apricot jelly

1 tbsp orange juice

4 small scoops vanilla ice cream

Method

1 Preheat the oven to 350°F/180°C/Gas Mark 4. Slice the top off each brioche and reserve, then carefully hollow out the centers and discard. Place 3 apricot halves in the middle of each brioche.

2 Put the brioches and their tops onto a baking sheet and cook for 8 minutes or until heated through and slightly crispy. Meanwhile, gently heat the jelly in a saucepan with the orange juice, stirring, until melted.

3 Place each brioche on a plate and top with a scoop of ice cream. Drizzle the conserve or jelly mixture over, then replace the tops.

Serves 4

Date Puddings with Sticky Toffee Sauce

Ingredients

3 oz/85 g butter, softened,
  plus extra for greasing

3¹/₂ oz/100 g pitted dates, chopped

3¹/₂ oz/100 g soft light brown sugar

¹/₂ tsp vanilla essence

2 large eggs

3¹/₂ oz/100 g wholemeal flour

1¹/₂ tsp baking powder

1 very ripe banana, mashed

Toffee Sauce

3 oz/85 g soft dark brown sugar

2 oz/55 g butter

2 tbsp light cream

Method

1 Preheat the oven to 350°F/180°C/Gas Mark 4. Grease 4 x 7 fl oz/200 mL pudding basins or ramekins with butter. Cover the dates with boiling water and soak for 10 minutes to soften.

2 Beat the butter, sugar, and vanilla essence until pale and creamy. Beat in the eggs, then fold in the flour and baking powder. Strain the dates and blend to a purée in a food processor, or mash with a fork. Stir into the mixture with the banana.

3 Spoon the mixture into the basins or ramekins, almost to their tops, and place on a baking sheet. Bake for 20 minutes or until well risen and just firm to the touch. Cool for 5 minutes, then loosen the puddings with a knife and invert onto plates.

4 To make the sauce, place the sugar, butter, and cream in a saucepan and heat gently for 5 minutes or until syrupy. Pour over the puddings to serve.

Serves 4

Plum Tart with Crumble Topping

Ingredients

7 oz/200 g unsweetened pastry, defrosted if frozen

14 oz/400 g plums or damsons, halved and stoned

3 tbsp superfine sugar

1 tsp cornstarch

2 oz/55 g chopped mixed nuts

2 tbsp demerara sugar

2 tbsp fresh breadcrumbs

Method

1 Preheat the oven to 375°F/190°C/Gas Mark 5. Roll the pastry out thinly on a lightly floured surface and line a 8 in/20 cm loose-bottomed flan tin. Refrigerate for 10 minutes, then line with baking paper and dried beans. Cook for 15 minutes, then remove the paper and beans and cook for another 5 minutes or until lightly golden. Cool for 5 minutes.

2 Meanwhile, put the plums or damsons into a saucepan with 4 tablespoons of water and the superfine sugar. Cook gently, covered, for 5 minutes or until the fruit is soft. Blend the cornstarch with 1 tablespoon of water. Stir into the fruit mixture and cook for 1 minute or until the juices thicken slightly.

3 Place the plums, cut-side up, along with any juices, in the pastry case. Mix together the nuts, demerara sugar, and breadcrumbs and sprinkle over the fruit. Bake for 15 minutes or until the topping is golden.

Serves 6

Pear and Almond Flan

Ingredients

2 large, firm pears, peeled, cored, and sliced

1 tsp lemon juice

2 oz/55 g superfine sugar

7 oz/200 g unsweetened pastry, defrosted if frozen

3–4 tbsp apricot or plum jelly

2 oz/55 g soft margarine

1 medium egg

2 oz/55 g all-purpose flour

$1/2$ tsp baking powder

2 oz/55 g ground almonds

1 oz/30 g flaked almonds

confectioners' sugar to dust

Method

1 Preheat the oven to 375°F/190°C/Gas Mark 5. Toss the pears with the lemon juice and 1 teaspoon of the superfine sugar.

2 Roll the pastry out thinly on a lightly floured surface and line a 8 in/20 cm loose-bottomed flan tin. Refrigerate for 10 minutes. Line the pastry with baking paper and a layer of dried beans and cook for 15 minutes. Remove the paper and beans and cook for another 5 minutes or until lightly golden. Leave to cool for 5 minutes.

3 Spread the jelly over the pastry and top with the pears. Beat the margarine and remaining sugar until pale and creamy, then add the egg, flour, baking powder, and ground almonds and beat to a soft, dropping consistency. Spoon the mixture over the pears, sprinkle with the flaked almonds, and cook for 30 minutes or until set and golden. Cool for 10 minutes, then transfer to a plate and dust with confectioners' sugar.

Serves 6

Broiled Peaches with Ricotta

Ingredients

6 ripe free-stone peaches

2 oz/55 g amaretti biscuits, roughly crushed

7 oz/200 g low-fat ricotta

1 tbsp superfine sugar

2 tbsp fresh breadcrumbs

Method

1 Cut each peach in half from top to bottom and, using both hands, twist to loosen the flesh from the stone. Carefully remove the stone with the point of a knife.

2 Place the peach halves, cut-side up, in a shallow flameproof dish. Divide the amaretti biscuits among the peach halves and top each with a large spoonful of ricotta.

3 Preheat the broiler to medium. Broil the peaches for 5 minutes or until the tops are lightly browned, then sprinkle with a little sugar. Increase the heat and broil for another 2 minutes or until the sugar browns slightly.

Serves 4

Ginger and Pear Steamed Pudding

Ingredients

5 oz/145 g butter, softened,
plus extra for greasing

5 oz/145 g light muscovado sugar,
plus 1 tbsp to coat

3 ripe pears, peeled and cored,
1 chopped, 2 sliced

3 pieces preserved stem ginger,
chopped, and 5 tbsp syrup
from the jar

2 large eggs, beaten

6 oz/170 g all-purpose flour

1 1/4 tsp baking powder

2 tsp ground ginger

1 oz/30 g fresh white breadcrumbs

finely grated zest of 1 lemon

Method

1 Grease a 5-cup-capacity pudding basin with butter and coat with 1 tablespoon of sugar. Carefully line the base and sides of the basin with the pear slices, then drizzle over half the ginger syrup.

2 Beat together the butter and sugar until light and fluffy, then gradually beat in the eggs. Sift together the flour, baking powder, and ground ginger, then fold into the butter mixture. Stir in the breadcrumbs, lemon zest, remaining ginger syrup, the stem ginger, and the chopped pear. Spoon into the basin and level the top, then cover the basin with a double layer each of baking paper and kitchen foil. Tie a piece of string around the rim of the basin to hold the layers in place, then cut off any excess paper and foil.

3 Place the basin in a saucepan and pour in boiling water to reach halfway up the basin. Bring back to the boil, then simmer, covered, for 1 1/2 hours, adding more water as necessary. Remove the basin from the water and leave to cool for 5 minutes. Invert onto a plate, tap the base, and remove the basin.

Serves 4

Rhubarb and Apple Crumble

Ingredients

8 oz/225 g rhubarb, chopped

2 tbsp fresh orange juice

2 tbsp sugar or to taste

butter for greasing

**8 oz/225 g eating apples,
cored and chopped**

Crumble

**2 oz/55 g chilled butter
or margarine, cubed**

3 oz/85 g wholemeal flour

2 oz/55 g porridge oats

2 oz/55 g soft light brown sugar

Method

1 Preheat the oven to 350°F/180°C/Gas Mark 4. Place the rhubarb, orange juice, and sugar in a saucepan. Cover and cook for 4–5 minutes, until the rhubarb begins to soften. Place the mixture in a lightly greased 9 in x 6 in/23 cm x 15 cm ovenproof dish, then stir in the apples.

2 To make the crumble, rub the butter or margarine into the flour with your fingertips, until the mixture resembles coarse breadcrumbs. Mix in the oats and brown sugar, then sprinkle over the fruit mixture. Bake for 40–45 minutes, until the topping is crisp and golden.

Serves 4

Index